DIVING AND SNORKELING GUIDE TO

Southern California

Including **Los Angeles County**
Orange County
San Diego County

Second Edition

Darren Douglass

Pisces Books™

ACKNOWLEDGMENTS

The sea is His, for He made it, and His hands formed the dry land.
—Psalm 95:5

Publisher's Note: At the time of publication of this book, all the information was determined to be as accurate as possible. However, when you use this guide, new construction may have changed land reference points, weather may have altered reef configurations, and some businesses may no longer be functioning. Your assistance in keeping future editions up-to-date will be greatly appreciated.

Also, please pay particular attention to the diver rating system in this book. Know your limits!

Copyright © 1994 by Lonely Planet Publications

Head Office: PO Box 617, Hawthorn, Vic 3122, Australia
Branches: 150 Linden St, Oakland, CA 94607, USA
10a Spring Place, London NW5 3BH, UK
71 bis rue du Cardinal Lemoine, 75005 Paris, France

First edition copyright © 1987 by Dale and Kim Sheckler.

All photographs by Darren Douglass.

Library of Congress Cataloging-in-Publication Data

Douglass, Darren.
Diving and snorkeling guide to southern California / Darren Douglass. — 2nd ed.
p. cm.
ISBN 1-55992-057-2
1. Skin diving—California, Southern—Guidebooks. 2. Scuba diving—California, Southern—Guidebooks. 3. California, Southern—Guidebooks. I. Title.
GV840.S78D66 1994
797.2′3′097949—dc20 93-20673
CIP

Printed in Hong Kong

Table of Contents

Sunsets at the beach at Little Corona can be spectacular.

How to Use This Guide

This second edition is designed to acquaint you with California's best beach diving sites from Los Angeles County to the Mexican border. Distant coastal reefs and island destinations are not contained in this publication—just some of the best dive sites available off California beaches.

Of California's expansive coastline, the area between Los Angeles and San Diego counties account for a lot of diving terrain—and a lot of divers because of the dense population. Welcome to suburban beach diving. Not all available dive sites are mentioned here because it would take several texts to contain them. This guide will focus on the best of the best, as well as tried-and-true favorites. Southern California is noted for its excellent beaches, but not all are suitable for diving. Each site included in this guide was chosen

Lingcod are common along Southern California's deeper, rockier reefs.

A diver is silhouetted on a small reef wall along the Orange County coast.

because of its consistently good visibility, variety of underwater flora and fauna, proximity to shore, and ease of access for divers. You may find yourself driving a distance to reach some of these locations, but weather permitting, the diving is worthwhile. There are enough excellent dive sites here to keep the most ardent diver busy for many weekends to come.

Remember that all diving areas are subject to oceanic and atmospheric conditions. All sites are effected by weather from time to time, but more often than not, you'll enjoy what you find beneath the waves.

Always evaluate dive site conditions and know your limitations. All dive areas listed in this guide require a degree of skill, but use common sense and good judgment if conditions preclude diving at your targeted site. Many areas involve rocky entries and/or incoming surf. Be wise in the estimation of your abilities as you plan your underwater adventures off Southern California's beaches.

Safe diving to you all!

Rating System for Divers and Dive Sites

A rating system (novice, intermediate, advanced) will be used throughout this volume. The reader needs to be aware that because of environmental conditions, an advanced site may resemble a novice site and vice versa. It is important to note that considerable beach and surf entry experience is desirable for anyone planning to dive off the shores of the Golden State. If you are visiting California and have not had this experience, you would be wise to venture seaward only on the calmest of days and in the novice areas. Completing an environmental orientation with an instructor or divemaster is highly recommended as well. It is assumed that any diver using this guide is in good physical condition.

A **novice diver** is defined as a recently certified diver without a lot of experience. In the same vein, this rating could also apply to a diver making his first California beach dive who is unfamiliar with the environment. An **inter-**

The docile angel shark can be found along many of the sandy dive areas along the Southern California coast.

mediate diver is one who has been certified over one year and logs 12 to 24 dives annually. An **advanced diver** does not necessarily have to have completed an advanced diving course, although it is certainly beneficial. In essence, an advanced diver has commensurate experience in many environments, including California beach diving. The individual may hold only an entry level certification, but should have logged 50 or more dives and feel extremely comfortable in all types of water conditions.

You will have to decide for yourself in which category you fit. A good diver will weigh his experience, evaluate water conditions, and make a proper assessment to dive or not. Venturing inside caverns or caves is suitable for those who have been trained and certified to execute these objectives. There are small caverns and caves located off local beaches. Beach divers can also reach significant depths. Some areas feature submarine canyons that can put divers in over 100 to 130 feet of water. Diving to these depths is considered beyond the realm of recreational divers.

A small sheepshead swims through a Southern California kelp bed.

A diver basks in a luxuriant kelp bed off the Point Loma area.

1

Overview of Southern California

This is the second edition of the *Diving and Snorkeling Guide to Southern California*. Specifically focusing on beach diving, this guide highlights the coast from Los Angeles to San Diego.

On any weekend, the Southern California coast can resemble a parking lot. Plan on arriving at your favorite dive site early, and don't forget quarters for the voracious parking meters. To be sure, uncrowded days do happen, but that's usually during the winter months or on weekdays. This volume will therefore describe several "little known dive sites" as well as the "populated" and popular areas.

Southern California offers numerous attractions for divers, including a Mediterranean-like climate and a changing shoreline dotted with numerous coves and isolated beaches. This region offers diving opportunities for all levels of divers.

Climate. Southern California is noted for its sunny weather, but many tourists associate sunshine with warm temperatures. Inland temperatures are warm throughout most of the year but along the coast, temperatures can become quite cool. If you'll be staying along the coast, bring along a warm jacket. From December to March, coastal temperatures range from 40–60°F. You should also carry an umbrella, as this is the rainy season in California. Temperatures rise slightly from April to early July, but expect fog and clouds during the morning and evening. From July to October, the weather is absolutely perfect—warm temperatures, clear skies, and clear waters. Although you can dive Southern California year round, the best time to dive is late summer and early fall. There are few storms and water visibility is generally good.

Southern California is well known for its sunny, pleasant climate as well as its versatile diving opportunities. Divers of all skill levels who enjoy wandering through majestic kelp forests, exploring the intricate reef systems, or just photographing the many colorful marine subjects will find great satisfaction diving along the Southern California coast. ▶

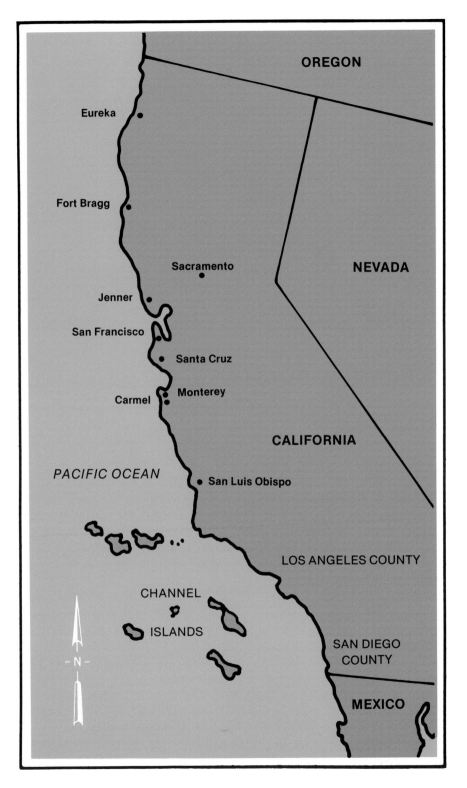

OREGON

Eureka

Fort Bragg

Sacramento

NEVADA

Jenner

San Francisco

Santa Cruz

Monterey

Carmel

CALIFORNIA

PACIFIC OCEAN

San Luis Obispo

LOS ANGELES COUNTY

CHANNEL

ISLANDS

- N -

SAN DIEGO
COUNTY

MEXICO

7

Diver's Cove and Picnic Beach are set up for convenient diving. The beach is wide and the reef system extensive.

Water Temperatures. Water temperatures follow the same cycle as air temperatures: 50–60°F in the winter and 60–70° in the summer. Deeper waters are obviously colder. With these water temperatures, you may want to wear a wetsuit. Some divers get by with a full-length tropical dive suit during the summer, but a full one-quarter inch wetsuit and hood are recommended.

Beach Diving. Beach diving has several advantages over boat diving: it's cheap and you can dive when you want and for as long as you wish. There are just a few guidelines to follow in preparing for a beach dive, and some diving techniques to keep in mind. Beach diving doesn't require a lot of physical strength, but you should have enough stamina to get in and out of the water, reach your offshore destination, and be able to handle an emergency. The best way to get in shape for beach diving is through some kind of aerobic exercise—running, cycling, dance, and swimming.

Try to schedule your dives for the morning. The sea tends to be calmer this time of day, and there are smaller crowds. Also try to plan your dives during periods of high or incoming tides. The incoming tides bring in the clear offshore waters, creating better visibility. The higher water may also help you get by a shallow reef on your swim out to the dive site. However, there are some limitations when diving during high tide. Some beaches may become impassable and the surf may be more difficult to handle.

Upon arrival at the beach, take time to carefully observe conditions. Use binoculars to scout out hidden reefs or kelp beds. Watch the surf carefully. Surf will often come in "sets" of two to five big waves, followed by about 10 minutes of small waves. Time these sets. Look for rip tides, which can get you offshore quickly. Carefully check entry and exit points and always have alternative entry/exit points in mind. Observe how the kelp is lying; this is a good indication of currents.

Waste no time entering the surf zone. Do not stop to adjust gear or look back. Swim out past the surf then rest. This will reduce your chances of get-

Entries can be made off rocky ledges, such as these at Diver's Cove, as easily as from sandy beaches. The technique is just slightly different.

ting knocked down. Should you fall, stay down. If the water is deep enough (2–3 feet), kick out the rest of the way. Many experienced divers wade out to this depth and turn to swim. Take the larger waves by going underneath them. If you time your entry properly and don't stop in the surf zone, you probably won't have any problems.

To exit the water, simply reverse the process. Approach the seaward side of the surf zone as closely as possible and wait there. Relax and catch your breath. Again, time the waves. Head for shore between wave sets. Waste no time and don't stop. When you reach waist-deep water, stand up and back out, keeping your eye on the surf. If you get knocked down and can't get up, stay down and crawl in.

Kelp. Giant kelp beds, some extending up 100 feet from the bottom, are typical in Southern California. Kelp grows very quickly, creating dense submarine forests which harbor a variety of fish and invertebrates. Kelp is only hazardous if you don't know how to deal with it. Perhaps the most important thing to remember is that kelp breaks easily. To avoid becoming tangled, keep your dive gear—fin straps, knives, and other tools—close to your body. Keep enough air in your tank to surface clear of the kelp. And always stay close to your dive buddy, so he can help free you. If you must pass through kelp on the surface, do so by crawling and clearing a path in front of you. Most important, *don't panic.*

Hunting. California offers some of the best underwater hunting in the world. Succulent lobster, tender abalone, and game fish of all types can be gathered here. In all locations, strict game laws protect marine life. It's your responsibility to become familiar with the regulations and obtain the proper licenses. At local dive stores you can get information regarding fishing licenses and specific hunting regulations.

Dive Stores. There are many dive stores in Southern California, and some of them sponsor trips to local beaches, often free to divers. A complete listing of Southern California dive stores is included in the Appendix.

2

Diving in Los Angeles County

Once past the Ventura/Los Angeles County line, the traffic, congestion, and general bedlam of greater Los Angeles awaits. The good news is all of this ends at the waterline, allowing divers a brief respite from the crowds and cars.

There is a lot of beach in Los Angeles, but this portion of the diving and snorkeling guide will focus on some of the out of the way dive sites as well as some of the favorites. Be forewarned that to get away from it all in Los Angeles requires some hiking and gear hauling to get off the beaten path. For the most part, Pacific Coast Highway is your road map. Shortly beyond the county line is Harrison's Reef, a decent dive site for the hardy swim-

Purple sea urchins are a common sight along the rocky reefs, especially near shallow, intertidal areas.

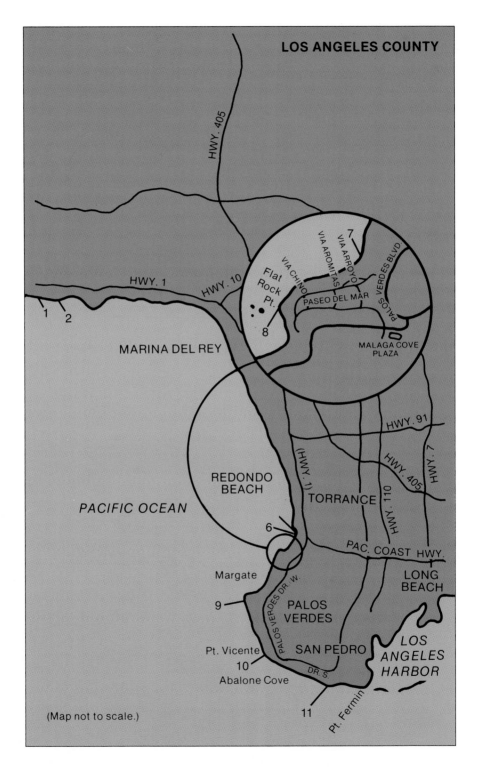

LOS ANGELES COUNTY

HWY. 405

HWY. 1

HWY. 10

1 2

Flat Rock Pt.

8

VIA CHINO

VIA AROMITAS

VIA ARROYO

7

PASEO DEL MAR

PALOS VERDES BLVD.

MALAGA COVE PLAZA

MARINA DEL REY

HWY. 91

HWY. 7

HWY. 405

HWY. 110

(HWY. 1)

TORRANCE

REDONDO BEACH

PACIFIC OCEAN

6

PAC. COAST HWY.

Margate

LONG BEACH

9

PALOS VERDES DR. W.

PALOS VERDES

SAN PEDRO

LOS ANGELES HARBOR

Pt. Vicente

10

Abalone Cove

DR. S.

11

Pt. Fermin

(Map not to scale.)

12

mer. With a few exceptions, the water is a little murky prior to the Palos Verdes Peninsula because of the clay run off that mixes with the water. But reefs are prolific, and offshore kelp beds abound. Although not exactly a photographer's paradise, Los Angeles County does provide excellent game-taking opportunities. Halibut are found in the sandy flats, while lobster and other marine life thrive on the offshore reefs. Two of the best-known areas for divers are Westward Beach and Point Dume, where a deep water submarine canyon brings in clear water and pelagic marine critters including squid and several varieties of shark. The area is known for its strong afternoon longshore currents, so it is best to dive it in the morning.

Bright colors are common along the Southern California coastline. Many colorful species enjoy posing for photographers.

◀ *Divers visiting the Los Angeles area will find excellent kelp diving off Sequit Point near Leo Carillo State Beach (1). Areas farther south offer good diving as well, but access may be more difficult. Other dive sites along the Los Angeles coast include El Matador Beach (2), Westward Beach (3), Point Dume (4), Paradise Cove (5), Sapphire & Pearl Street/Veteran's Park (6), Malaga Cove (7), Flat Rock (8), Christmas Tree Cove (9), Point Vicente Fishing Access (10), and White Point (16).*

Typical depth range:	10–45 feet
Access:	36000 Pacific Coast Highway; campsites on mountainous side of road
Water entry:	Sand and rocky beach
Snorkeling:	Good
Rating:	Novice to intermediate
Visibility:	15–25 feet

One of the largest kelp beds along the Southern California coast lies just 20 yards off Leo Carillo State Beach. The shoreline runs east to west, with two sandy beaches separated by the rocky Sequit Point. A giant kelp forest anchors itself to the rocky reef with pencil-thin strands that form the holdfast. Clusters of fronds spread in dense tangles, supporting a large population of marine life including urchins, starfish, anemones, nudibranchs, mollusks, and small sponges. Photographers should explore the rocks under the kelp beds for the best photos of marine creatures, and don't forget to look on the outer edges of the reefs for colorful gorgonians.

An underwater photographer and a gorgonian get to know each other better.

Christmas tree worms are a great bet for photographers on just about any Southern California reef. Even if visibility is less than fantastic, an underwater photographer working with a macro system can do well.

Hunters will find a few small lobster, abalone, and rock scallops concealed under the rocks. The kelp beds also shelter a wide variety of game fish, including kelp bass and sheepshead. Halibut can be spotted on the sand between the reefs.

You can access the beach to the west of the point but, during the winter months, a storm can sometimes wash out the road that leads to the beach. There is a good side to the winter storms; the road closure keeps the crowds away. If the road is open, there is a fee for day use and camping.

Your best bet is to park on the seaward side of the highway near the "Mulholland Highway" sign. It's just a short walk down a gentle slope to the entry-exit areas on the point. Immediately to the west of lifeguard tower #2 and to the east of tower #3 is a stairway that leads to sandy coves located between the rocks. These are good areas for entries and exits. The enormous kelp bed starts about 20 yards from shore and extends a quarter mile out. Rips and currents can be unpredictable, so observe conditions carefully. Lifeguards work during the summer and on some holidays; it's best to check water conditions with them before getting wet.

There are some rocks in the surf, but these shouldn't pose a problem as long as you note their position before entry. The bottom drops off moderately. Although the kelp is abundant, in most locations it's not thick enough to obstruct underwater passage. On the bottom, the reefs rise 10 feet in some spots. An occasional tall boulder can be found covered with feather worms, anemones, and other interesting invertebrates.

The diving area at Leo Carillo is large. You can enter the water from the beaches on either side of the point. Despite their close proximity, each beach offers a different experience to divers. It would take several dives just to begin exploring the special attractions of the area.

Typical depth range:	25–35 feet
Access:	32359 Pacific Coast Highway; parking lot and picnic tables with stairs to beach
Water entry:	Stairway to sand and rocky beach
Snorkeling:	Fair
Rating:	Intermediate to advanced
Visibility:	10–15 feet—better when Santa Ana winds blow offshore

Four beaches to the south of Leo Carillo—Nicolas Canyon (not a state beach), El Pescador, La Piedra, and El Matador—offer good diving without the crowds that congregate at Leo Carillo. El Matador Beach is the southernmost beach in this string of state beaches. El Matador is located off Pacific Coast Highway (Highway 1), approximately four miles south of Leo Carillo and two miles north of Transcas Beach. You'll find ample parking, restrooms, and picnic tables. The park is open from 8 a.m. to sunset; no overnight camping is allowed. There is a day-use fee which you pay at a self-service box located on the side wall of the outdoor toilets. There's no running water.

Beach diving often requires long walks or hikes with heavy equipment. Beach divers must take care not to overexert themselves on the way to the site.

A blood star and stone coral occupy the crest of a rocky reef.

A moderately steep path leads to the beach. The path is broken up by two sections of stairs, which together amount to about 80 steps. Before descending the steps, take a few minutes to take in the beauty of the beach. Almost directly off the beach is a reef with rocks that break the surface. The reef extends out about 75 yards in depths of between 10–20 feet. Although kelp grows here, visibility can be reduced by surge. Snorkeling is also good when the surf is low. Looking out past the shallow reefs, you'll see another kelp bed 75–150 yards out. These reefs offer the best diving, with depths ranging from 25–35 feet. Large kelp beds extending along the shoreline in both directions create a huge diving area that will satisfy divers at all skill levels.

Most of the reefs consist of very large boulders on a sandy, rocky bottom. Some boulders rise 15 feet from the bottom, displaying clusters of gorgonian, corynactis, and giant keyhole limpets. While there are other sites in Southern California better suited to macrophotography and sightseeing, El Matador offers ample variety of color and marine life to pique anyone's interest. Watch for the Garibaldi, senoritas, and even a few bluebanded gobies darting about.

Underwater hunters will find sheepshead, rockfish, and kelp bass. Halibut can sometimes be seen on the sand surrounding the reefs. Although the game fish in this area aren't particularly large, the quantity is sufficient. Among the selection are lobster and a limited number of abalone. Scallops can also be found.

Conditions at El Matador vary because the beach is exposed to weather. A day or two of pounding surf or rain can reduce visibility considerably. On good days, visibility averages 10–15 feet, though it can reach 30 feet on calm winter days or when the Santa Ana winds kick up. Currents don't pose much of a problem and usually only affect the outer edges of the kelp beds.

Typical depth range:	25–65 feet
Access:	If driving north, take left turn on Westward Beach Road, small rocky reefs at base of Birdview Road
Water entry:	Sand beach
Snorkeling:	Poor
Rating:	Intermediate to advanced
Visibility:	15–25 feet or better

Normally considered a surf spot south of Zuma Beach, Westward is a sandy oasis with a few scattered finger reefs. On uncrowded days, divers can park right along the sand and make a short trek to the water. Westward is a favorite

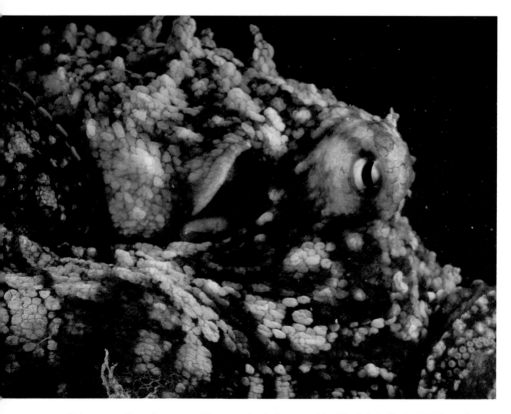

Octopus are found among pilings, under ledges, and inside debris that might have been discarded by fishermen. Although shy, they will usually hold still for an approaching photographer.

Tube anemone tentacles make interesting close-up subjects, and you'll find them just about everywhere.

for dive kayak launching and is a happy hunting ground for corbina, halibut, and surf perch. Stay clear of surfers by diving near the small wash rocks. Westward drops off deep fast, leading into the submarine canyon at Point Dume. Shorebreak can be fierce, but with proper timing divers can make a beach entry and be in deep water quickly by ducking under the waves.

The good news is that once you are in six feet of water or more the surge dies down because most of the waves break directly on the beach. Watch out for the surf fishermen because a treble hook won't go well with your wetsuit. Divers will find sand dollars, sea pens, sand stars, and bat rays. Just because the area is mostly sand, don't think there is nothing there. Observe closely and you'll probably find sea mice, hermit and spider crabs, octopus, and a variety of small shellfish making their way through the sand. A lot of diving instructors conduct checkout exercises here on calm days.

Typical depth range:	25–90+ feet
Access:	Enter gate directly next to Westward Beach Road, pay entrance fee, and drive all the way to deadend by bluffs
Water entry:	Sandy beach
Snorkeling:	Fair
Rating:	Novice to advanced (depending on conditions)
Visibility:	10–35 feet or better during upwelling

A short distance down the road from Westward Beach, Point Dume offers uncrowded sand, ample parking, and restroom facilities beneath the shadow of a 200-foot monolithic headland. This is a great place to bring a picnic lunch and make several dives. The rocky point ends at the base of the bluff and cascades seaward into the deep waters of a submarine canyon. The sandy beach near the rocks can place the unwary beach diver in over 100 feet of water quickly, but constant monitoring of depth gauges and/or dive computers will avoid this. The rocky reefs dissipate as the water gets deeper, leaving a large sandy plain that is home to bat rays, pacific electric rays, and migrating grey whales. An extensive sand dollar bed is encountered at 40 feet, as are large crabs. Because of the steep dropoff near the submarine canyon, Point Dume is a favorite habitat for mating squid. After a "squid run" it is not unusual to encounter massive plumes of white squid eggs waiting to hatch. When this occurs, blue sharks and bat rays come in as if someone rang the dinner bell.

Longshore currents are strong here when afternoon winds pick up, so be sure to evaluate the site before plunging in, unless you want to get swept around the corner into Paradise Cove. This is unadvisable because it's a long and difficult walk back. But when divers gauge currents properly, Point Dume offers some of the best sand diving in Los Angeles County. It is also a favorite "hang out" for migrating grey whales who rub their skin against the sand to dislodge barnacles and parasites.

One final note of caution: Point Dume is a great dive site for novice divers provided they correctly assess the conditions. When the current is running and shorebreak is steep, even advanced divers consider moving elsewhere. If you're not sure, check with the lifeguards.

Orange is just one of the hues of this multi-tone anemone. Corynactis is the most common specimen found in Southern California. ▶

Typical depth range:	15–50 feet
Access:	Enter gate directly off Hwy 1
Water entry:	Sandy beach (a few exposed rocks at lower tides)
Snorkeling:	Fair
Rating:	Novice to intermediate
Visibility:	5–15 feet

Paradise Cove does not rate high with many local divers because visibility is occasionally marginal and reefs are sometimes not encountered until divers crash into them. But the shore facilities are excellent, and the diver willing to plumb the murky depths will find an abundance of marine life.

Paradise is often used as a checkout site for diving classes. This is a privately owned beach with a restaurant and 200-foot pier. Parking is plentiful and close to the water's edge. There is a fee to enter the cove, but freshwater showers near the picnic area are worth the expense at the end of a dive. In the 1970s Paradise Cove was used as a set for the television series *The Rockford Files,* starring James Garner.

Small colorful invertebrates are abundant in Southern California for those who take time to observe the subtleties of local reefs.

There are remnants of an artificial reef in 50 feet of water. In the late 1950s, the California Department of Fish and Game sank over 20 old automobiles as fish aggregating devices.

Until divers swim out into deeper water, the terrain at Paradise Cove consists largely of sandy bottom. On the few rocky finger reefs, divers may encounter lobster, an elusive abalone or two, and a variety of marine invertebrates. Halibut can be found in the sand flats.

Divers swimming far from shore will encounter a deep water kelp bed that flourishes beyond the cove's entrance. It's a pretty reef, although water clarity is usually marginal, but there is a greater concentration of marine life here because the site is not regularly visited except by shore-based divers using dive kayaks. Boat traffic can be heavy here, so exercise caution.

An orange Garibaldi investigates some gorgonian sea fans.

Typical depth range:	15–110 feet
Access:	Take Hwy 1 to Pearl Street, lots of parking adjacent to Veteran's Park
Water entry:	Sandy beach
Snorkeling:	Fair
Rating:	Novice to intermediate
Visibility:	10–35 feet

Around the turn of the century, Redondo Beach was the hub of Los Angeles' maritime trade. Redondo Canyon, a deep offshore submarine canyon, enabled merchant ships to come in close to shore when the seas were calm. In the late 19th century, piers were erected off the beach to service the growing merchant trade. The area quickly became a popular vacation spot for residents of nearby Los Angeles, who could be seen strolling the piers or watching ships bringing cargo from the Northwest and Far East pull into port.

In time, three piers were built. Pier #1 stood at the foot of Emerald Street. It was destroyed in 1914 by a violent storm, but has since been rebuilt into the famous "Horseshoe Pier." Pier #2 was a Y-shaped pier located at

Winter mornings are usually clear on the beaches at Sapphire and Pearl streets, Redondo Beach.

Ainsworth Court, next to Veteran's Park (then the luxurious Redondo Hotel). It, too, was heavily damaged by a storm in 1915 and was eventually torn down. The 480-foot Pier #3, located at Sapphire Street, met a similar fate in 1926. By that time, the shipping boom at Redondo Beach was nearing an end, as a new port was being constructed at San Pedro. Redondo Harbor is beyond the present-day pier. Since boat traffic can be busy at times, a flag and float is recommended.

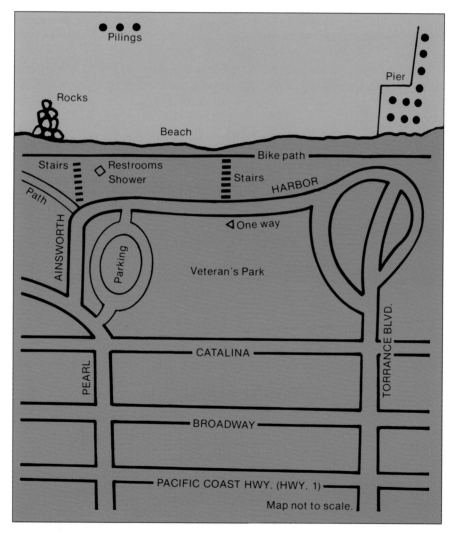

Historic Redondo Beach in Los Angeles is the site of late 19th-century piers built to service merchant ships. Some of the piers were destroyed by storms, and they are now considered to be spectacular dive sites.

All that remains of Pier #2 are three broken pilings, located just beyond the lip of the canyon less than 80 yards from shore in 45 feet of water. All are within 10 feet of each other and lie parallel to the shore and canyon. Colorful anemones adorn the pilings and tiny shrimp and an occasional octopus can also be seen nearby. From the pilings, the canyon drops rapidly to about 70 feet and then moderately to greater depths. To the north, the canyon walls are slightly steeper and drop to as much as 90 feet before tapering off. Stay well to the south of the existing pier, because it's illegal to dive on or near the pier.

Although the canyon isn't as spectacular as the La Jolla Canyon in San Diego, just to peer into the darkness from the edge can be an exhilarating experience. As you might expect, the water here is clear and cold. Visibility averages 15–20 feet, but during upwellings, visibility of 40 feet is possible.

An abundance of marine life can be found on the sandy and muddy bottom. At the edge of the canyon and along the canyon slope, sea pens poke from the sand and blue-gray spiny sand stars make their way across the bot-

The California spiny lobster (Panularus interuptus) *is a welcome sight for divers when lobster season opens.*

Spanish shawl nudibranch (Flabelonopsis iodenia) can be found on local reefs. They are also found in kelp beds.

tom. In the canyon, you may see an octopus hiding in a discarded jar, crabs amidst the debris, and an occasional lobster crawling from the depths.

To reach the park, head west on Torrance Boulevard. Turn left on Catalina Avenue. A parking lot is located at the intersection of Esplanade and Catalina, south of the Elk's Club and Veteran's Park. Turn right on Esplanade to get into the parking lot. There's plenty of metered parking to the south and west of Veteran's Park. Don't forget to bring plenty of quarters for the meter.

A stairway leading to the beach is located at the west end of the lot. Restrooms and showers are situated at the base of the stairs. Water entry is easy if the surf is low. Because of the canyon, surf is usually two feet lower than at other beaches nearby.

Marine photographers can find excellent opportunities off Southern California beaches.

The 460-foot Pier #3 off Sapphire Street was the busiest of the piers at Redondo Beach in the early 1900s. A railroad which carried cargo to and from the merchant ships ran to the end of the pier. There was also a restaurant owned by The Pacific Steamship Company at the end of the pier. While only three pilings remain of Pier #2, there are still many artifacts from Pier #3 to be found.

Among these artifacts are more than 20 pilings that rise as much as 12 feet from the bottom. The pilings are covered with beautiful pink anemones which make interesting photo subjects. You may also recover a few bricks and broken dishes from the restaurant. If you're lucky, you may even find a bottle or a dish bearing an insignia.

To reach the area, take Pacific Coast Highway (Highway 1) and turn west on either Sapphire or Topaz in Redondo Beach. Both of these streets end at the Esplanade. Park along the street and take the path between the buildings at both locations to get to the beach. Water entry is just north of the jetty. Facilities include showers and restrooms.

Water entry is generally easy in light to moderate surf. The sandy bottom slopes gently to approximately 35 feet about 100 yards from shore. This is where remnants of the pier pilings can first be spotted. To get to the pier, swim on the surface outward from the beach to just beyond the jetty. You should be directly out from the second set of condominiums situated north of the jetty. Many divers locate the wreckage by swimming northwest across the bottom at a 45 degree angle from the end of the jetty. Don't be discouraged if you miss the wreckage on first try. The pier area is long and narrow and it's very easy to swim too far north, south, or too close to shore.

Look for the bricks scattered on the bottom and you're in the area. Simply fan the bottom with your hand to uncover broken fragments of dishes. The broken pilings here are short and often covered with kelp. Depending on the weather, the kelp may reach the surface at some locations, indicating the location of the dive site.

The tall pilings are seaward and at the southern edge of Redondo canyon in about 40–45 feet of water. The canyon begins to drop off moderately north of here. If, in your search for pilings, you find yourself dropping into the canyon, you've gone too far to the north. Move up the sloping bottom and head south. The pilings are positioned about 15–25 feet apart so you have to move around to spot all of them. The outermost pilings are about 200 yards from shore.

Ocean conditions at this dive site are generally very good. Visibility averages 10–20 feet. Upwellings from nearby Redondo canyon can increase visibility to 30 feet. Surf is little or no problem, particularly during the summer months when the beach, which faces west, is well protected from the predominantly southerly swell. Prevailing westerlies during the winter can occasionally bring big surf, while currents are almost nonexistent. The only real hazard facing divers is the boat traffic from nearby Redondo Beach, so a flag and float are recommended.

Hunting in the area is generally limited to halibut, which are often taken in the sand surrounding the pilings. At times you can spot a small kelp bass. Sculpin and cabezon have been known to frequent the area. Other marine life include the comical and slow-moving sheep crab, octopus, sea pens, and sea pansies.

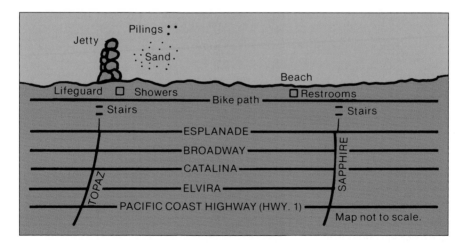

Pier #3 was one of the destroyed Redondo Beach Piers that serviced merchant ships at the turn of the century. The main attraction these days is the sunken pilings, now overgrown with sea life. On shore, facilities include restrooms and showers.

Typical depth range:	10–35 feet
Access:	Paved path off Paseo Del Mar
Water entry:	Sandy beach with rock to south
Snorkeling:	Good
Rating:	Novice to intermediate
Visibility:	10–35 feet

Malaga Cove lies where the long sweeping beaches of the Los Angeles South Bay end and the rocks and cliffs of Palos Verdes begin. This makes for an interesting bottom of sand, rocky reefs, and kelp beds. Lobster aren't uncommon in the rocky areas, but most aren't very big. Considering the good access to Malaga Cove, these waters hold a fair amount of game, including kelp bass (around the kelp beds) and halibut on the sand. For those who don't mind a long swim, you'll find rock scallops farther out.

For photographers and sightseers, diving Malaga Cove will show you marine life not common at other dive sites around Palos Verdes. Don't be surprised if you come across an angel shark buried in the sand. Some divers claim they've spotted angel sharks as long as five feet! Also look

Colorful marine life thrives in the reefs and ridges that make up Flat Rock. The kelp and unusual reef formations support an excellent variety of fish and anemones.

Perch and gorgonian sea fans are abundant in the area.

closely in the rocks for horn shark, octopus or sheep crab. These and other creatures—bat stars, ochre stars, nudibranchs, gorgonians, and Garibaldi— are also present.

To reach Malaga Cove, exit Pacific Coast Highway in Redondo Beach to Palos Verdes Boulevard south. You'll pass through a portion of Torrance before reaching Palos Veres Estates. The road bears east before heading to the west, passing in front of the beautiful Malaga Cove Plaza. Turn right on Via Corta, which turns into Via Almar. Turn right at Via Arroyo in front of the Malaga Cove School. This will lead you to Paseo Del Mar. The parking lot will be on the right. After parking, proceed to the gazebo that overlooks the cove from the cliff above. From this vantage point you'll get a good indication of water conditions below.

A paved path leads to the beach. It's a moderately steep but short path. If you have a cart you can wheel your gear down to the beach and suit up there. There are two areas from which to enter the water. Where you enter will depend on personal preference and water and weather conditions. The first is from the rocks adjacent to and in front of the swimming pool. The second is from the beach. Entering from the rocks shortens the swim to the outer kelp beds considerably, but can be hazardous in moderate to heavy surf. The water immediately in front of the rocks is shallow. High tide is the best time to enter from the rocks. Many divers prefer to enter at the sandy beach and swim out to the edge of the reefs. But watch out for surfers here.

Although visibility averages 12 feet, conditions at the cove vary considerably. The cove is vulnerable to westerly and northwesterly swells. Under these conditions, it's recommended that you head to the other side of the peninsula. Runoff from rain can also affect visibility. Diving conditions are superb and visibility can reach 25 feet if winds are from the south or if the Santa Ana winds are blowing.

Sun worshippers should head to Torrance Beach (adjacent to the cove), where there are fewer crowds compared with other beaches on the South Bay.

Typical depth range:	25–40 feet
Access:	Dirt path off Paseo Del Mar
Water entry:	Rocky reef
Snorkeling:	Excellent
Rating:	Intermediate
Visibility:	15–40 feet

Many divers agree that the west side of Palos Verdes offers some of the best coastal diving in Southern California. However, many of the sites are difficult—if not impossible—to access. The exception is Flat Rock Point, located where the coastline at Palos Verdes swings to the south.

Here you'll find good diving on an interesting sea bottom. The bottom drops off quickly from shore to depths of 25–35 feet. The terrain consists mostly of boulders and reefs that run in ridges and rise 5–10 feet. Between the ridges, small patches of ivory sand create clearings in the thick kelp beds that blanket the area. The lush kelp and unusual reef formations support an excellent variety of marine life. Numerous Garibaldi, senoritas, kelp bass, sheepshead, and other varieties are present. There are few species of game fish, with the possible exception of large halibut that pass over the small sand patches between the reefs.

Hunters will no doubt delight in the large population of lobster here. Many of the reefs near the shoreline have been picked clean of the larger "bugs." A few can still be found in the shallows and even in very deep water. Abalone are slowly making a comeback, thanks to the efforts of local divers who've agreed not to hunt them here.

A diver stops to observe gorgonian sea fans.

The tube anemone comes in a variety of colors.

Photographers and sightseers should enjoy the usually good visibility, which averages 15–20 feet. Colorful nudibranchs, starfish, gorgonians, and anemones make their home on the bottom. Other invertebrates, including an abundance of sea cucumbers, keyhole limpets, and sea hares, are also present. Look in the reef crevices for yellow and black striped treefish, small (and shy) bluebanded gobies, and an occasional horn shark. Urchins are common, so watch those knees!

Shore access to the point is difficult but not impossible. Flat Rock Point is located down the road from Haggerty's and Malaga Cove. Proceed to the area via Pacific Coast Highway. Once you reach the city of Torrance, exit to Palos Verdes Boulevard south. Follow this to the town of Palos Verdes Estates, past the Malaga Cove Plaza. Turn right on Via Corta, which turns into Via Almar as it bears to the left. After passing Via Arroyo, Via Aromitas, and Via Media, you'll come to Paseo Del Mar. Turn left. The head of the trail leading to Flat Rock Point will be directly ahead, where the road rises sharply and begins to curve to the left at 600 Paseo del Mar.

The trail to the beach begins as an old dirt road (sorry, no vehicles permitted). The trail breaks off to a moderately steep dirt path. Avoid the trail after a rain because the path can become muddy and very slippery. Even when dry, the trail can be treacherous, so proceed with caution.

The trail ends at the flat rocks on the point. Depending on the size and direction of the surf, entry is from the rock where depths drop sharply to 12 feet. Experience in this type of entry and exit is recommended. Under the right surf conditions, there are some small coves in the rocks to the northeast of the point that can also be used.

Typical depth range:	10–45 feet
Access:	Dirt path off Paseo Del Mar
Water entry:	Rock and boulders
Snorkeling:	Excellent
Rating:	Intermediate
Visibility:	15–40 feet

The reefs at Christmas Tree Cove are quite spectacular in some spots. In one location, a large section of the reef—the size of a bus—juts 18 feet from the bottom and drops vertically to a kelp bed below. Other areas of the reef are marked by overhangs, channels, and huge boulders. Lush kelp beds surround the reefs. Christmas Tree Cove has the best water visibility in the area. Averaging 15–25 feet, visibility rarely drops below 10 feet and can be as great as 35 feet.

The thick kelp and rugged bottom terrain inhabit a wide variety of sea life, including sponges, anemones, starfish, mollusks, the giant keyhole limpet, turban snail, kellet's whelk and brown chestnut cowrie. Red and blue Spanish shawl and bright yellow sea lemon nudibranchs provide interesting splashes of color here and there. You'll also see opaleye, rock wrasse, Garibaldi, and hundreds of senoritas swimming above and around the reefs.

Rose anemones are a colorful addition to Southern California beach diving reefs.

Scores of California spiny lobsters await the determined lobster hunter from October to March.

Look for the striped treefish in crevices and the tiny and colorful bluebanded goby darting about.

Game fish are also plentiful, though not as abundant as in other areas off Palos Verdes. Halibut are sometimes found on the sand that surrounds the kelp, as are kelp bass, sheepshead, and a small population of rockfish. You may also find some scallops and lobster. Keep in mind that it's illegal to take abalone from the area.

The only drawback to this site is the poor shore access—a steep dirt path along the north side of the cove. Only the sure-footed diver should attempt this route. And exercise caution after a rain; the path can become slippery and muddy. To reach the path, take Pacific Coast Highway to Palos Verdes Drive West. Follow this road south for approximately five miles (you'll drive through the town of Palos Verdes Estates). Turn west on Paseo Lunado. The road turns into Paseo Del Mar as it swings along the coast. The foot of the path is located in the 2800 block of Paseo Del Mar near the intersection of Paseo Del Mar and Via Neve. There's limited but ample street parking. There are no facilities.

Ocean conditions can be easily observed from the top of the bluff. After proceeding down the steep trail, water entry can be made through the surf at the stone and gravel beach in the center of the cove. Or, if conditions permit, you can enter from the rocks on either side of the cove. It's a long swim through thick kelp to reach the best reefs on the outer edges of the kelp. There are some interesting reefs and kelp beds closer to shore.

35

Typical depth range:	20–50 feet
Access:	Steep dirt trail off Paseo Del Mar
Water entry:	Rock and boulders
Snorkeling:	Good
Rating:	Intermediate
Visibility:	15–40 feet

Local divers have come to accept the difficult shore access at many of the dive sites around Palos Verdes. Point Vicente, nicknamed "Cardiac Hill," is no exception. But it's really not as bad as it sounds. The steep trail is located to the west of the Point Vicente lighthouse. There's adequate parking. Restrooms and a drinking fountain are located at the top of the trail. "Cardiac Hill" is long and steep but fairly safe. Diving along the shoreline at the bottom of the hill is worth the effort.

Rockfish are common along most of the Southern California coastline.

A gorgonian sea fan and sea star are found together on this shallow reef.

The beach between Point Vicente and Long Point is fairly large and offers a wide diving area. The best location is to the east, at the end of the branch of the trail that heads toward a small rocky point. The east branch is a little narrow in some spots but visibility is best here. And, depending on conditions, entries are easiest from this spot.

By contrast, entry over the rocks can sometimes be difficult. It's fairly easy to enter and exit from the sandy beach in the center of the cove. But this results in a long swim to reach the clearest waters to the east. Before descending the trail, determine the conditions and your diving goals to choose the best entry/exit point and dive spot.

The bottom drops off gradually to 50 feet just 150 yards from shore, eventually leveling to a sandy bottom. Most of the reefs consist of boulders of varying sizes. Some are large and extend to within 10 feet of the surface, creating large caves and overhangs that are exciting to explore. If water visibility is good, you can sometimes spot these large boulders from the cliff top.

Visibility in this area is fair, averaging 10–15 feet. The best visibility is usually on the east side of the cove, which is somewhat protected from northwest swells but susceptible to southerly swells during the summer. The bottom is covered mostly with silt which can reduce visibility during heavy surf. Close to shore, strong currents aren't usually a problem, but near Point Vicente, currents have been known to reach two knots.

Marine life near the rocks is not as abundant as in other areas around Palos Verdes, but there is certainly enough variety for sightseers, photographers, and hunters. Expect to see giant keyhole limpets and nudibranchs and, on the ledges and overhangs, corynactis anemones. Numerous strands of gorgonians add color to the deeper waters. Sea hares and sea cucumbers are also common in deep waters. Fish life includes Garibaldi, senoritas, opaleye, and halibut. There are a few scallops and lobster as well. Kelp cover on the reefs is patchy. If the kelp growth is heavy you can expect more game moving in the cove. Hunting for abs is strictly prohibited here.

Typical depth range:	15–45 feet
Access:	Park entrance off Palos Verdes; driveway down the cliff and park
Water entry:	Rock and boulders
Snorkeling:	Poor
Rating:	Novice to intermediate
Visibility:	5–10 feet

White Point is the only location along the Palos Verdes Peninsula where you can drive right down to the water's edge. Thousands of divers have taken their first dive here and, although this location is considered a beginner's spot, divers of all skill levels will find something of interest.

Prior to World War II, the local Japanese-American community built a bathhouse here over natural hot water vents. Remains of this bathhouse are visible just above the high tide mark, but the hot water vents are only visible underwater. The vents are located on the rocky bottom close to shore (the nearest vent is less than 25 yards out). They're identified by the strange white fungus that surrounds them. You can actually feel the warm water rising from some of the larger vents. If your hands get cold while diving, simply run your fingers through the warm sand at the vents.

Diving in the surrounding area is, quite frankly, not as spectacular and beautiful as in other areas along the peninsula. But there are some interesting features. The shallow waters offer plenty of scenery for the novice snorkeler. Beyond this area, there are reefs that extend off the points to the north and south, forming overhangs, crevices, and small caves. Approximately 150 yards out, three reefs run parallel to each other, separated by sandy patches. Here, in 35–45 feet of water, is the best diving around. The offshore reefs are, however, best left to more experienced divers who can handle the longer swim and currents.

Starfish (including the colorful bat star), ochre star, and many nudibranchs (particularly the beautiful orange and blue Spanish shawl) can be found on the reefs. Other invertebrates here include a variety of anemones, sea cucumbers, giant keyhole limpets, and, in deeper waters, gorgonians. At one time there was an underwater nature trail, but heavy storms in recent years have destroyed it. There are plans to rebuild it.

For the photographer there are also some morays, but surprisingly few Garibaldi. Fish populations have been depleted over the years, but some species are making a comeback. Lobster can be found on reefs located in deep water. Abalone, particularly black abalone, are making a slow comeback, *but hunting abalone is prohibited.* Sheepshead, halibut, and kelp bass are available on the deeper reefs, while perch and opaleye reside in shallow waters.

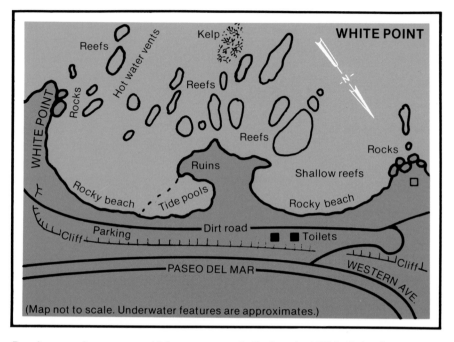

Beach access is as easy as driving your car onto the beach at White Point. Spectacular sights in this area include the ruins of a pre-World War II bathhouse on shore and the hot water vents on the ocean bottom not far from shore.

Years ago, a ship wrecked on the point and broke up. Subsequent storms broke the ship into tiny pieces and spread them over a wide area. Look closely for brass nails and other small items.

Conditions at White Point are usually good. Visibility on the reefs averages 10–15 feet. Conditions on the deeper offshore reefs can be somewhat better. The small cove where most divers enter is protected from weather most of the time, but conditions can be hazardous on the rocks at high tide.

To reach White Point and nearby Royal Palms State Beach, proceed south along Western Avenue through the town of San Pedro. The road will swing to the left and join with Paseo Del Mar. The road to the point is located less than one block away at 1800 W. Paseo Del Mar. It's the only road that leads to the water and, though unmarked, it's hard to miss. There is sometimes a $3 day use fee for the state park (Royal Palms), depending on the time of year and time of day. Proceed down the hill and bear left until the road turns to dirt. A small cove is approximately 100 feet ahead. Park on the side of the road. Most divers enter from the cove, which is just a few steps from the water's edge. Some divers prefer to enter off the rocks at either point, but this is recommended only for experienced divers. In the cove, enter the water from the rocks.

3

Diving in Orange County

In the late 1960s and early 1970s, the Orange County coast was a sleepy seaside area. Development was nearly nonexistent and agriculture boomed throughout the region. Beach access was virtually unlimited. You could park along Pacific Coast Highway and venture to its sand and rocky shores.

But times have changed. Industry moved into the area. A population boom ensued, and fences, gates, and parking meters sprung up along Highway 1. Today, parts of industrial Orange County feature a small skyline. Even Huntington Beach, Surf City, USA, resembles neighboring Los Angeles. Despite the growth, the cars, the mass of humanity flocking to the beaches, there are excellent diving sites off the Orange County coastline, considered by some to provide the heaviest concentration of sandy beach and rocky cove diving in Southern California.

From Huntington Beach to South Laguna Beach, a plethora of dive sites await. If you are diving on the weekends, you may consider arriving early to find available parking spaces. The terrain is diverse with sandy flats, small caverns, finger reefs, underwater archways and surge channels. Kelp is not as prevalent as it is in other places, but is making a comeback in the Laguna Beach area.

Recently Crystal Cove State Park was formed. It takes a healthy hike to get down the cliff to the beach, but it is usually uncrowded even in the summer. Divers should be aware of surfers in the area, because surfers and divers tend to use the same reefs. Water clarity is often excellent, making Orange County a mecca for divers. Another good feature of the site is the numerous coves that face different directions. If a swell renders one site undiv-

Orange County is well known for its good beach diving. Facilities in the diving areas of Orange County are usually well-equipped, and water entries are generally safe and easy. Dive sites include Huntington Beach (12), Newport Beach Pier (13), The Wedge (14), Big Corona Breakwater and Reefs (15), Little Corona (16), Crystal Cove State Park (17), Pelican Point (18), Crystal Cove (19), Scotchman's Cove (20), Crescent Bay (21), Shaw's Cove (22), Fisherman's Cove (23), Diver's Cove (24), Picnic Beach (25), Rocky Beach (26), Wood's Cove (27), Cleo Street (28), Moss Street (29), Aliso Beach County Park (30), and San Juan Rocks (31). ▶

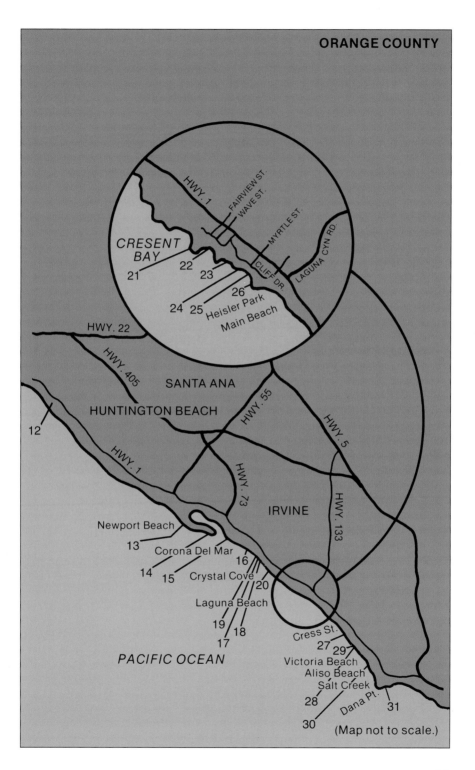

ORANGE COUNTY

HWY. 1

FAIRVIEW ST.
WAVE ST.
MYRTLE ST.
CLIFF DR.
LAGUNA CYN. RD.

CRESENT BAY

21   22   23

24   25   26
Heisler Park
Main Beach

HWY. 22

HWY. 405

SANTA ANA

HUNTINGTON BEACH

HWY. 55

HWY. 5

12

HWY. 1

HWY. 73

HWY. 133

IRVINE

Newport Beach

13

Corona Del Mar

14   15   Crystal Cove

16

20

Laguna Beach

19   18

17

PACIFIC OCEAN

Cress St.

27   29

Victoria Beach
Aliso Beach
Salt Creek

28

30

Dana Pt.

31

(Map not to scale.)

41

able, a short drive to a westerly or southwesterly facing cove will yield good diving results. The diving here is not very deep, but diverse marine flora and fauna add to the undersea beauty of Orange County. Mile for mile of coastline, Orange County offers great diving opportunities close to shore.

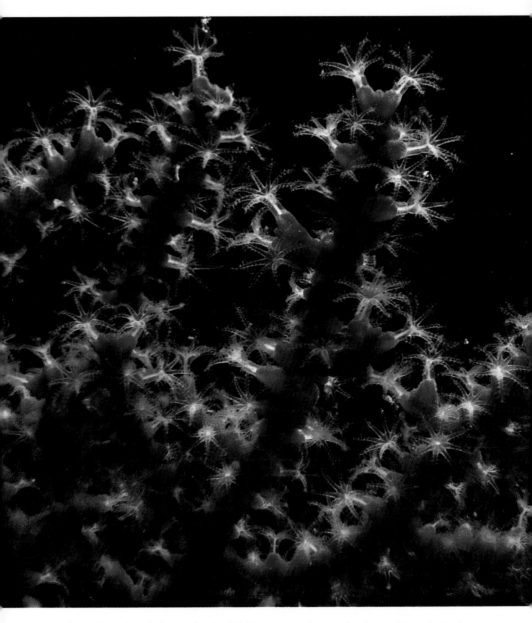

An underwater photographer backlights a gorgonian sea fan for a different effect.

Typical depth range:	10–20 feet
Access:	Park south of Huntington Pier off Pacific Coast Highway
Water entry:	Sand and surf
Snorkeling:	Poor to fair
Rating:	Novice—Intermediate
Visibility:	5–20 feet

This is a "sleeper" dive site. The area is all sandy plains and reefs are absent. Don't let this discourage you however, because the observant eye can find a lot to see and enjoy in the "Sahara" of dive areas.

The area is predominantly shallow. Pismo clams are often found just beyond the surf line. Divers can easily bring back a game bag of large clams just by drifting along in the prevalent longshore current with an abalone iron and digging these seagoing delicacies out of the sand. They are easily identified by the V-shaped bivalve wedge that protrudes a few inches out of the sandy bottom. Just remember where you entered the water—chances are the longshore current will carry you several lifeguard towers northward depending on wind and swell conditions.

Divers will also encounter the occasional octopus, halibut, and shoals of corbina and surf perch. During winter months when upwelling increases water clarity and brings plankton and baitfish closer to the shallow, dolphins are usually found feeding from the Santa Ana River Jetty to Huntington Cliffs.

Diving off Huntington Beach is different and uncrowded and provides a rewarding change of pace.

A surfer shreds the waves at an Orange County beach. Divers should give board riders a wide berth.

Typical depth range:	10–20 feet
Access:	Pier parking lot off Balboa Blvd.
Water entry:	Sand and surf
Snorkeling:	Not recommended*
Rating:	Novice–intermediate
Visibility:	10–25 feet

This is a different type of diving area. It is best during winter months and during periods of offshore breezes that cause upwelling of clear water. Usually lifeguards discourage diving the pier in the summer because of the heavy fishing, swimming, and boogy board traffic. Summer south swells will make diving here dangerous.

This is another sandy area, but with one difference: pier pilings. Marine encrustation along these wooden structures is fabulous. Small anemones, barnacles, and starfish make excellent photo subjects. At the base of the pilings, divers will find tube anemones growing in the sand, as well as a contingent of spider crabs, corbina, perch, and hermit crabs. If you look carefully, you'll find sea mice. These fuzzy looking V-shaped cousins to sea urchins slowly scurry along the sandy bottom. Divers can gently pick up these strange little creatures for closer observation. They are sand colored and appear to have no eyes (they don't have tails like land mice). These hapless denizens of the sandy plains are content to scavenge for scraps of food and bait that fall from the pier. Bat rays and sand sharks forage for food here as well.

Underwater hunters may encounter sand bass, halibut, and sole. Not far beyond the outskirts of the Newport Pier is a submarine canyon that drops to depths of hundreds of feet. Occasionally deeper water creatures migrate vertically and move close to shore. Pelagic jellyfish and barracuda can commonly be observed, as well as schools of jack mackerel. One interesting note: In 1986 a 17-foot great white shark was "hooked" by a commercial fishing boat not far from the pier. Don't be alarmed as this is an extremely rare occurrence, but if you feel like staying close to the pilings and away from open water areas, you may be more comfortable.

Diving closer to the pier is a good idea as well if anglers are present. Because the fishermen tend to cast their lures out away from the pier, diving beneath the pier is wise. And there is no telling what you may find. This place is a treasure trove for lost fishing poles, tackle boxes, expensive lures, and lead weights. The Newport Pier offers interesting marine life as well as "treasure" of sorts.

---

* Lots of fishermen cast from pier. It would not be pleasant to be "hooked."

Sheepshead go through various coloration stages in life: a tannish yellow as juveniles, soft rose as adolescents, and bright red and black (male pattern) as adults.

Typical depth range:	5–20 feet
Access:	Street parking off Balboa Blvd.
Water entry:	Sand and surf
Snorkeling:	Not recommended
Rating:	Advanced
Visibility:	15–25 feet

The Wedge is an infamous spot on the north side of the Newport Breakwater that is known for its bone-breaking high surf during south swells. Here, a wedge-shaped peak is formed when incoming swells meet outgoing backwash. When it breaks, strong surf explodes in very shallow water. But the breakwater is calm during winter months. Whatever you do, evaluate conditions first.

The site is divable when calm and is a good place for lobster night dives. Lobsters inhabit the breakwater rocks and a hunter can do quite well during season. The good news is that lobster season is during the winter, and conditions can be calm. Surfers go out here, and the Wedge is a popular spot for boogy boarders and body surfers. There is a submarine canyon shortly

Marine forest biostructure thrives at the Wedge in Newport Beach. The forest is doing well thanks to the volunteer efforts of the Marine Forest Society.

beyond the jetty. Sometimes visibility can exceed 25 feet during offshore wind conditions.

A special man-made "marine forest" is located a short distance off the Wedge's shores as well. This forest is a series of plastic, floating "biostructures" that have been anchored into the sand bottom by volunteer divers from the Marine Forest Society. Originally intended to attract kelp holdfasts, these huge suspended columns have attracted colonies of mussels, barnacles, nudibranchs, and shoals of fish. Other structures made of old net and plastic tubing have been transformed into fish habitats. The Marine Forest project is a great example of how volunteer divers working with the State of California can enhance offshore fisheries resources.

Be careful to evaluate the swell before going in the water near the Wedge. The combination of shallow water, surge, and strong surf can make the Wedge a wicked wave break to be avoided. When diving is good however, go for it. Just be sure to watch the tide. Incoming tides can change conditions quickly.

A bright orange Garibaldi swims by a vibrant red gorgonian fan.

Typical depth range:	15–25 feet
Access:	Ocean Blvd & Iris Avenue; driveway to entry gate
Water entry:	East end of Newport Breakwater with rocks farther east; lots of sand in between
Snorkeling:	Good on south side
Rating:	Novice
Visibility:	10–30 feet

Big Corona is an excellent facility for divers. Parking is abundant, there are restroom and fire pit facilities, and surprisingly good diving. The breakwater helps keep the waters calm (storm swells excepted) and there are small reefs directly in front of the parking lot. A more extensive, shallower reef system exists to the south. The "sleeper" here is the sand patches between the reefs. To the naked eye this is another great desert of sandy plains. Those who are familiar with the area know better. In the swimming area (roped off with buoys so neighboring Newport Harbor boat traffic steers clear), is

Snorkeling at Big Corona is always a pleasurable experience. The shallow reefs are an aquatic refuge to small lobster and black abalone.

a series of small reefs in 15–25 feet of water. These reefs feature small contingents of scallops, gorgonian sea fans, anemones, and shoals of surf perch and corbina, as well as the ever present Garibaldi.

The calm waters at Big Corona make it a site often frequented by diving instructors and their students. The flat sand bottom is an excellent platform for performing skills and training exercises, and the reefs are great for guided tours. Easy access, freshwater showers, and food concessions (during the summer only) make Big Corona a site well worth the price to park. There is one other benefit: In the winter, parking attendants occasionally are not on duty. Parking is free!

Overall, Big Corona is a big area with much to offer. It is also great for night diving. A roaring fire on the beach welcomes nocturnal divers pursuing lobster along the breakwater and reefs.

A diver examines a blacksmith. These fish are found on reefs throughout Southern California.

Typical depth range:	10–30 feet
Access:	Ocean Blvd. & Poppy Avenue; paved trail leads to beach
Water entry:	Sand and boulders
Snorkeling:	Excellent
Rating:	Novice to intermediate
Visibility:	10–30 feet

Experienced divers often avoid crowded dive spots, assuming that the best dives lie in some remote area below steep cliffs. Little Corona, however, is one of those popular spots where, if you can deal with the crowds, you're in for some spectacular diving.

Located in the southern corner of Newport Beach less than a mile south of the mouth of Newport Harbor, Little Corona attracts a fairly steady crowd. But divers keep coming back, and with good reason. There's plenty of marine life and terrain to interest divers at any skill level. Large halibut can be found in the sand and horn sharks can be seen cruising the reefs. Although the supplies of game fish have been diminished over the years, there's still an adequate selection of fish, including lobster, kelp bass, and rockfish.

Little Corona also offers some unusual scenery for the sightseer and photographer. On the reefs, in depths of 20 feet or more, expect to find gorgonians, starfish, feather worms, and other invertebrates. Visibility here is generally good; on the outer reefs, visibility averages 15 feet–30 feet under the best conditions. Closer to shore, visibility can be reduced due to water turbulence over the sand, but it's usually good enough over the shallow reefs in calm weather for snorkeling.

Divers should not let the crowded beach of Little Corona keep them from diving this area. An abundant variety of marine life thrives among the reefs offshore.

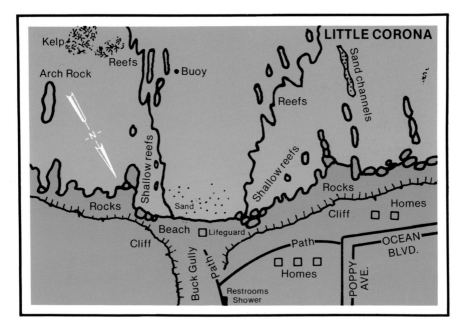

◄ *Corynactis anemones are also known as strawberry anemones.*

The reefs start in shallow water and, approximately 150 yards out, slope down to 30 feet. Some of the shallow reefs are covered by a thick blanket of eel grass. The middle of the cove is mostly sand, but there are numerous small rocks in the surf line that can trip you up during entry and exit. The reefs lie on either side of the sandy cove. The most interesting reefs are located to the south about 100 yards out. A buoy in this area directs boats to stay clear. Other intriguing reefs lie just seaward and to the south of this buoy. Further down the coast is the unusual Arch Rock that rises from the water and usually hosts several species of birds. Despite the buoy directing boats to stay clear, the area is very close to Newport Harbor. For this reason, it is recommended that you use a flag and float.

Also keep in mind that this area is part of the Newport Beach Marine Life Refuge. It's illegal to remove any marine life other than normal game.

Little Corona can be reached by turning south onto narrow Poppy Street off East Coast Highway (Highway 1) in Newport Beach. Poppy Street deadends at a point that overlooks the sea, then turns sharply onto Ocean Boulevard. There's limited free parking on Ocean Boulevard. The path to Little Corona is to the left of this intersection. A moderately steep paved path winds down to the beach. Restrooms and showers are located halfway down the path, tucked in a corner to the left.

A close look reveals that many California marine creatures, such as this gorgonian, are made up of complex and simple patterns. Expect to find excellent photographic subjects and good visibility at Little Corona.

Typical depth range:	15–70 feet
Access:	Parking lots on both sides of PCH with paved paths, stairs, or dirt trails leading to the beach
Water entry:	Sand and small rocks
Snorkeling:	Good
Rating:	Intermediate to advanced
Visibility:	15–35 feet or better

There have been significant developments and changes along the rural stretch of Pacific Coast Highway from Corona Del Mar to Laguna Beach. This was once an area where divers could park on the highway and trek down trails to the beach. Now highway parking is prohibited in most of the area, and paved parking lots (with their usual entrance fees) have arrived. Despite this, the encompassing area still remains undeveloped compared to most of Orange County, and hopefully will remain that way for good.

Sunlit kelp forests await a short swim off local Southern California beaches.

A diver examines a bright orange Garibaldi on a South Laguna Beach.

Prior to 1979, all of this land belonged to the Irvine Company. Because most of the ranching and agricultural endeavors ignored the shore line, the land was acquired by the State of California. The sprawling stretch of beach called Crystal Cove State Beach is composed of many small beaches such as Pelican Point, Reef Point, and Scotchman's. There are more dive sites, but these are the most popular. These three will be listed separately.

All of Crystal Cove State Park's shore line and nearshore waters are encompassed by the Irvine Coast Marine Refuge. The park is Orange County's largest stretch of undeveloped coastline.

Divers hike down trails, small beaches, and pocket coves that bear no formal name and, even in the height of summer, can find themselves on an isolated beach by Orange County standards. After making a beach entry, divers will soon find themselves swimming over numerous finger reef systems graced with large colorful gorgonian sea fans. Moray eels inhabit rocky structures, as well as lobster, bass, and bright orange Garibaldi. These oversized damselfish are territorial by nature, and will "attack" divers who come too close to their nests. Fortunately attack only means making bluffed charges at the divers. After several runs, the Garibaldi will retreat in irritation. Divers may take lobster and fish in the marine refuge, but tide pool and other intertidal organisms must be left alone. Garibaldi may not be taken in California. It is a protected species because of its tropical coloring. Many divers argue that the Garibaldi need no protection because they inundate local inshore water south of Point Conception. It's just as well, that they can't be taken because most hunters consider damsels poor tasting fish.

Throughout the park area, a dedicated hunter can obtain large specimens of halibut, occasional white sea bass, and sheepshead. A 40-pound plus sheepshead was taken with a polespear in Crystal Cove waters before the fish became more wary of speargun-toting divers.

Typical depth range:	15–60 feet
Access:	Park on PCH, trek down cliff
Water entry:	Sand and small rocks
Snorkeling:	Good
Rating:	Intermediate to advanced
Visibility:	15–35 feet or better

This is one of the best dive sites available south of Corona Del Mar. It requires a hike down a marine terrace, but is usually worth the effort because it's uncrowded.

As with most of the dive sites located within Crystal Cove Park, finger reefs abound with crevices, gorgonian fans, and a sparse representation of kelp. Garibaldi, small sheepshead, rock wrasse and sea stars abound. The reefs extend several hundred yards off shore, but depths rarely exceed 50–60 feet. The dive is somewhat predictable. There are numerous finger reefs interspersed with sand. Divers with a seaward compass heading will jump from reef to reef with sand patches in between.

Colorful sea stars are found here, and deeper depths are often fished by commercial lobster trappers as noted by the buoys marking the lobster cages. One word of caution: If you see a lobster caged in a trap, don't even think about breaking it out for yourself. The fines for poaching are still and hell hath no fury like that of a robbed lobsterer. Find your own under a rock-pile. It's the sensible thing to do.

The sea lemon is a colorful member of the nudibranch/droid family.

Typical depth range:	15–45 feet
Access:	Park on PCH and trek in the private road just before the Sunshine Shake Shack
Water entry:	Sand and small rocks
Snorkeling:	Good
Rating:	Intermediate to advanced
Visibility:	15–35 feet and better

In the 1940s a small wood cottage community arose at Crystal Cove proper, and still remains. Coastal access is permitted by foot only, but it is worth the long walk. Crystal Cove itself is not often dived.

The entry is predominantly sand, unless winter storms erode the beachfront and expose small rocks. A small kelp bed sits in front of the Sunshine Shake Shack (a great place to enjoy a date shake while evaluating conditions. A small rocky promontory and reef mark the southern end of the beach. The typical finger reefs are not prevalent here, and terrain ranges from sand bottom to tall rocky reefs.

This is a favorite site for breath-hold spearfishermen because white sea bass and halibut visit the area during the fall and spring months.

The reef itself is covered with colorful sea stars and anemones, as well as nudibranchs and iridescent Christmas tree worms. If you are a diver who likes to get away from the coastal crowds, Crystal Cove should be on your underwater itinerary.

Corynactis anemones and barnacles are a colorful addition to Southern California beach reefs.

Typical depth range:	10–45 feet
Access:	Pull into Reef Point parking lot and use the stairs to access the beach
Water entry:	Sand and small rocks
Snorkeling:	Good
Rating:	Intermediate to advanced
Visibility:	10–35 feet

The region marks the end of Crystal Cove State Beach. At the southern end of the beach is Scotchman's Cove, also known as Scotty's. Reef Point is an extensive offshore wash rock connected by a finger reef system. Divers can pick either area: Reef Point or Scotchman's (closer to the El Morro trailer park on the beach). Both areas will not disappoint, provided conditions are favorable.

In the short history of sport diving, Scotchman's Cove has earned a solid reputation for its superb game fish population. Although the supply of game fish has diminished over the years, many beach divers still consider Scotchman's Cove a reliable hunting area. You'll discover lobster at depths of 30 feet and sometimes in the shallows among the eel grass. Scallops are also available, but usually in outer waters. Abalone are present in small numbers but it's illegal to take them. The most abundant species include calico, kelp bass, and sheepshead. Other fish can be found, but the heavy spearfishing activity in this area has scared off many species of fish.

Scotchman's Cove is also a good spot for underwater photography and sightseeing. The bottom drops off quickly to 10–20 feet. Several shallow reefs covered with eel grass make this an excellent area for snorkeling during calm weather. The deeper and more intriguing reefs lie 100–200 yards out. For the best sightseeing and game fish, stay close to the exposed offshore reef. In addition, there are large reef formations rising 20 feet from the bottom in some spots. These create immense walls of rock on which you'll see gorgonians, starfish, and anemones. There are plenty of crevices, cracks, and overhangs to explore, as well as the patches of sand that separate the reefs. Ribbon kelp grows from the rocks. Most of the larger kelp beds are gone, but may grow back in the near future.

Visibility is generally good, averaging 10–15 feet. During the winter months, visibility can reach 20–30 feet. The area is open to heavy surf, which can reduce visibility when large swells roll in. But perhaps the most salient features of the area are the excellent facilities that have been installed recently on the bluff overlooking the beach. Scotchman's Cove lies at the southern end of Crystal Cove State Park. Many of the park's facilities have recently undergone renovation. New restrooms and freshwater showers and sinks have been installed. Several new paved parking spaces have also

been added. Because the cove lies within park boundaries, there's an entrance fee charged at the gate.

To reach Scotchman's Cove, take Highway 1 to Laguna Beach. Follow the signs marked "Reef Point" to get to the gate. The path and stairs that lead to the beach are located just beyond the new restrooms on the bluff. The path is moderately steep but safe. You can get a bird's eye view of the diving area from the bluff. A large reef that extends from the point is located up the coast and to the right. Diving is good on both sides of the reef but, as always, weather, surf, and currents will determine the best diving area. Entry from the sandy beach is through surf. Keep in mind that the area is open to swells and should be avoided during periods of heavy surf.

Typical depth range:	20–70 feet
Access:	Turn right off PCH at Cliff Drive and take stairs down to beach
Water entry:	Sand entry
Snorkeling:	Good to excellent
Rating:	Novice to advanced
Visibility:	15–45 feet

This is a unique area. The southern end near Shaw's Cove has surge channels that traverse into the neighboring cove. A diver can progress in 15 feet of water through a labyrinth of small canyons and exit at the other end. The northern end of the beach has an extensive reef system too, covered with Spanish shawl nudibranchs, scallops, and a variety of anemones. The northern reef system is beautiful, but requires an additional walk.

Advanced divers can make the long swim to Deadman's Reef, located in front of the northern reef section. It's a healthy swim out, but divers can traverse the sandy plain at the end of the inshore reef and, with an accurate seaward compass heading, come across a tall reef system that juts from 50 feet to a height of 15 feet of water. The seaward side of the reef cascades

Giant kelp beds create dense submarine forests that harbor a variety of fish and invertebrates.

into the sand at a depth of 70 feet depending on the tide. This is a beautiful reef adorned with anemones, scallops, mussels, and barnacles. Large varieties of fish congregate here as well, including perch, calico bass, opaleye and sheepshead. Rockfish thrive here also. Because of the many fish congregating in the area, recreational anglers usually anchor boats over the reef. While watching out for bobbing lures, a diver can surface swim in the direction of the boat and descend nearby, saving air in the process. Just be sure to keep an eye out for moving boat traffic. Dive flags are not required, but can be useful when diving Deadman's.

Finally, the section between the northern reef and southern reef hosts a wide expanse of sand. This is a great place for spearfishermen to search for halibut. Sightseers will encounter rays, leopard and angel sharks. Crescent Bay has a little bit of something for everyone.

Typical depth range:	20–50 feet
Access:	Stairway off Cliff Drive near Fairview Street
Water entry:	Sand and rocky entry
Snorkeling:	Good to excellent
Rating:	Novice to intermediate
Visibility:	10–50 feet

Welcome to one of the most popular dive spots in Laguna Beach. Nearly every weekend it's not uncommon to see two or three classes using the cove for checkout dives. And don't be surprised if you see several buddy teams emerge from the water with smiles on their faces. Beach diving conditions here are as close to ideal as you're going to get along Laguna Beach. The crowds are perhaps the only drawback to the area, but don't let them turn you away from an otherwise superb dive site.

The cove is well protected from wave action. Consequently, the surf averages less than two feet. Currents are weak or nonexistent and the visibility is rarely below 15 feet. In fact, it often exceeds 35 feet.

Given these conditions, it's no wonder the cove is popular with diving instructors. Students can learn surf and rock entries and exits under mild conditions, and excellent snorkeling is also available.

The bottom terrain is both interesting and varied. On the western side of the cove, the rocks extend out from the point and drop rapidly to the sand in 20–35 feet of water. A 15-foot channel at the end of the point starts at 20 feet and cuts deep into the reef. To locate the "crevice," as it's called by local divers, swim seaward on the bottom along the edge of the rocks. The crevice begins as a 15-foot cut into the reef and extends to the west. The crevice then narrows to a tunnel that's filled with Garibaldi and other marine life. Eventually the crevice branches off into smaller channels and tunnels, where you'll find octopus that can be hand fed. A note of caution: The crevice is affected by surge and strong currents. Experienced divers will benefit from these conditions, as the surge helps direct visitors in and out of the channels. Underwater activities can be observed from the rocks at the surface directly above the crevice at low tide. Farther out along this reef in deeper water, gorgonians can be found attached to the rocks. Friendly Garibaldi are more abundant here. Nudibranchs and a variety of anemones add color to the area.

Game fish are sparse in Shaw's Cove, probably because of the number of divers who come here. Expect to find an occasional morsel on the outer fringes of the reef. You can take most game fish in the area but, because Shaw's Cove is part of the Laguna Beach Marine Life Refuge, there are some restrictions. Be familiar with the hunting regulations before you dive.

Diving on the eastern side of the cove is less spectacular but far less crowded. A shallow reef covered with blade kelp and eelgrass extends out

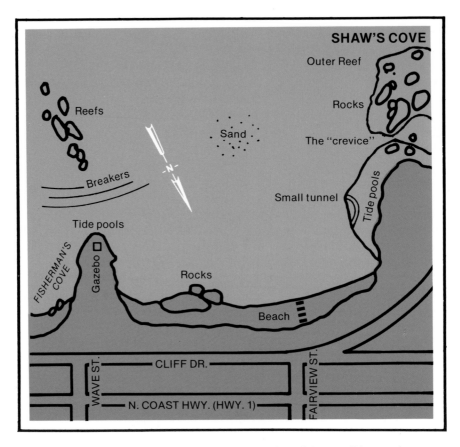

SHAW'S COVE

Outer Reef

Rocks

Reefs

Sand

The "crevice"

Breakers

-N-

Small tunnel

Tide pools

Tide pools

FISHERMAN'S COVE

Gazebo

Rocks

Beach

WAVE ST.

CLIFF DR.

FAIRVIEW ST.

N. COAST HWY. (HWY. 1)

A very popular dive site, Shaw's Cove offers near-perfect diving conditions and average visibility. Divers of all abilities enjoy this spot because of the varied terrain and sea life.

approximately 100 yards from the eastern point. At several places the reef rises 8 feet above the bottom. Gorgonians and anemones cover the walls here. On the far side of the eastern reef, there's a shallow channel filled with a variety of fish and, in one particular crevice, two huge moray eels.

Shaw's Cove is located between two other favorite Laguna Beach dive sites—Crescent Bay to the north and Fisherman's Cove to the south. A short walkway and stairway leading to the cove are located at the end of Fairview at Cliff Drive, a block from the North Coast Highway (Highway 1). Street parking is limited, so it's best to arrive early on the weekends. If your schedule permits, you can miss the crowds by visiting Shaw's Cove during the week. Be aware that the area surrounding the cove is privately owned. Trespassers are discouraged!

As for facilities, there's a dive store located a block south of Fairview at the intersection of Wave Street and Highway 1. A burger stand is located across the street from the dive store.

Typical depth range:	15–40 feet
Access:	Small stairway off Cliff Drive; south of Shaw's Cove
Water entry:	Sand and rocky entry
Snorkeling:	Good to excellent
Rating:	Novice to intermediate
Visibility:	15–45 feet

Fisherman's Cove, also known as Boat Canyon, falls within the Laguna Beach Marine Life Refuge. While there are some restrictions on the type of game that can be hunted, there are no restrictions on the most popular catch—lobster. And because the area isn't as well known as other sites nearby, game fish continue to be in good supply. In addition to lobster (found in the cracks and crevices), sheepshead, kelp bass, and halibut abound. The lucky diver may even find a large scallop or two on the rocks. Keep in mind that the reef on the southeast end of Fisherman's Cove extends into Diver's Cove, which is part of a marine/ecological preserve. It's illegal to hunt in this area. The boundary is marked by a crack in the point which divides Diver's Cove and Fisherman's Cove. To play it safe, stay well northwest of the point and enter and exit only at Fisherman's Cove if you're hunting.

Besides game fish, you'll also find some interesting reef formations—some of the best in Laguna Beach. One such reef is located about 75 yards off the small beach. Rocks can be seen from the surface of this reef, which extends shoreward to the southeast side of the cove. The reef rises from a sandy bottom and offers a number of deep channels, large crevices, and over-hangs to explore. The channel is located in 25 feet of water less than 60 yards from shore on the north edge of the reef. The channel varies in width from 10–20 feet, with walls that are 15 feet high. Farther out on the reef, the rock walls become quite steep, rising as much as 25 feet from the bottom. A few feet to the north, across the sand, are some medium-sized patch reefs. You'll find more channels and crevices on the seaward side of the reef and to the east.

For the sightseer and photographer, there are gorgonians on the reef, some kelp, a sizeable population of Garibaldis, senoritas, kelpfish, opaleyes, octopuses, nudibranchs, and an occasional moray eel. Diving conditions here are as good as those at Shaw's and Diver's Coves and, unlike neighboring areas, Fisherman's Cove is somewhat protected from the southerly swells. Diving on the north side of the reef offers some protection from surge generated by the southerly swells. Visibility averages 15–20 feet. Strong currents are unusual and generally affect the outer reefs.

To reach Fisherman's Cove, drive to Laguna Beach on Highway 1 and exit toward the beach at Cliff Drive, located one block south of the dive store.

The rocks in front of Condominium Point at Divers Cove make a great entry spot for divers when conditions are calm.

Follow Cliff Drive as it bears to the left. The stairway and path leading to Fisherman's Cove are located to the right of the Laguna Sea Cliff Condominiums/Apartments. Park on the street or in the metered spots in front of Diver's Cove. Showers and restrooms are located at Heisler Park, about 300 feet south of Diver's Cove. The beach is small and sometimes totally covered during high tide. Respect the privacy of residents.

Make your entry north of the reef. On the south side, between the outer rocks and the point, the reef comes very close to the surface, creating hazardous surf. North of the main reef is a sandy area and a shallow reef covered with eel grass. Within 20 feet of the shore, the bottom drops off quickly to 10 feet. To the north are shallow reefs that join up with the south end of Shaw's Cove. Some game fish and a wide variety of marine life can be found here. In the middle of this reef, in about 20 feet of water, is a wide crevice where two very large morays have been known to hide.

Typical depth range:	15–45 feet
Access:	Parking meters off Cliff Drive; directly next to condominiums
Water entry:	Sand and/or rocky entry
Snorkeling:	Good to excellent
Rating:	Novice to intermediate
Visibility:	15–45 feet

Yard for yard, this is probably one of the most heavily dived areas in Orange County—just be sure to bring enough change for the parking meters! It is a favorite for dive instruction classes because of the diversity of the terrain and easy access. Here you will find everything from sandy plains, finger reefs, surge channels, and small, but limited caverns. The surge channels are not as predominant as they are in neighboring Shaw's Cove, but they are fun to visit nonetheless.

Because of the diversity of the terrain and the abundant marine life (the southern end of Diver's Cove is the extreme boundary of the Laguna Beach Marine Life Refuge), thousands of divers receive their initial certification training in this area. Indeed, Divers Cove has often been dubbed the "check-out" capitol of California, and it may well be. Starting at 6 a.m. on weekend mornings, vans, trucks, and cars start pulling in as classes assemble on the beach. During summer months, a Laguna Beach City ordinance requires all dive classes to be off the beach by 10 a.m. That's the good news. Parking places open up and the beach crowd is thinned out considerably, creating a great time for already-certified divers to engage in an underwater sortie at Diver's Cove.

A sparse amount of kelp lies on the main reef section (north) in front of the condominiums (hence the name Condominium Reef). The thickness of the kelp has been affected by the coastal water mineral content and concentrations of bryzoan, so the kelp tends not to be as heavy as in years past. No game of *any kind* can be taken from Diver's Cove. This enhances its popularity among new divers seeking to observe species of sheepshead, senorita, rock wrasse, perch, and the occasional octopus. Small lobster can be found underneath ledges and inside crevices. Diver's Cove runs southward to its neighbor, Picnic Reef. Here, scuba divers will discover a slight change in terrain, as well as marine life just a short distance away.

Note: When the cove is calm, divers can carry their gear out onto the rocky area in front of the condominiums for rocky entry and exits. This is a great way to dive because gear will be free of sand. Just check with the lifeguards first. If there is a swell, this area may be closed off to divers due to the surge sweeping over it.

Typical depth range:	15–40 feet
Access:	Parking meters off Cliff Drive; follow stairway to sand
Water entry:	Sand and surf entry
Snorkeling:	Good to excellent
Rating:	Novice to intermediate
Visibility:	10–40 feet

The name of this dive spot suggests activities besides good diving. Be sure to pack a picnic lunch to enjoy between dives in the lush park on the bluff overlooking the beach. Restrooms, picnic tables, outdoor barbecues, and a freshwater shower are available.

Just off the wide and generally uncrowded beach a series of reefs stretch seaward more than 100 yards to depths of 40 feet or more. The reefs consist of a series of ridges that rise 10 feet from the sandy bottom. As you might expect, there are cracks, crevices, and overhangs to explore. In one spot there's a tunnel—too narrow for divers—that runs underneath a 20-foot reef. On your journey you'll see Garibaldis, senoritas, opaleyes, and bluebanded gobies. Colorful anemones, giant keyhole limpets, gorgonians, moon sponges, and Spanish shawl nudibranchs on the rocks provide perfect scenery for sight-

This ring spotted droid was found on a southern Laguna Beach reef.

A diver cavorts with a Garibaldi in a San Diego kelp bed.

seers and photographers. The kelp beds on the reef are plush but not too dense to obstruct passage.

Picnic Beach is located in a marine preserve. Consequently, hunters are not welcome and sightseers should take nothing but pictures. Visibility averages 15–20 feet; during the winter months, visibility can reach 40 feet.

The area is located south of Diver's Cove. Take Highway 1 to Myrtle. Myrtle ends at Cliff Drive. Metered parking is available along Cliff Drive. Bring plenty of quarters. Crowds can be a problem during the summer, so arrive early. The ramp to the beach is slightly to the right and through the park. The cove is somewhat protected, so entry is usually easy. Avoid the center of the beach as there are rocks in the surf that break surface at low tide. Kelp is sparse on the reef that lies close to shore in 25–35 feet of water. The thicker kelp to the south is more easily reached by entering at nearby Rocky Beach.

Typical depth range:	15–50 feet
Access:	Parking meters off Cliff Drive; follow stairway to sand
Water entry:	Sand and surf entry
Snorkeling:	Good to excellent
Rating:	Novice to intermediate
Visibility:	10–40 feet

The shoreline at Rocky Beach is varied, offering a number of entry and exit points. A huge kelp bed extends from 50–200 yards offshore. In the middle of this—approximately 100 yards from shore—a large reef breaks the surface at low tide. A number of smaller reefs surround the large one, creating a huge diving area that can accommodate a good crowd of divers without making anyone feel claustrophobic.

A wide selection of entry and exit points doesn't imply that entry is easy. The diver should have some experience with surf entries over rocks. Entries and exits will be somewhat easier if the surf is light or moderate.

Close to shore, the bottom drops quickly to 10–15 feet. There are many small low-lying reefs, sand patches, and channels. The shallow reefs are excellent for snorkeling when the surf is low, but diving with tanks here can difficult in moderate surf because of the surge. If you're using tanks, there's no reason to linger in the shallows because deeper water is just a short swim away. The larger reefs, particularly the one that breaks the surface at low tide, can be quite spectacular. At 20–30 feet, the reef walls drop vertically

Gorgonian sea fans are abundant in Southern California waters.

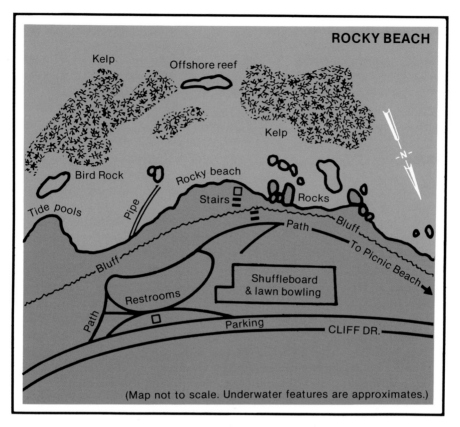

Many divers will find Rocky Beach to their liking, mainly because of the versatility of the area. There are many entry/exit points, and a large kelp bed lies within 200 yards of shore.

and then slope to depths of 40–50 feet. Kelp surrounds most of the area. Crabs, large anemones, and broad strands of gorgonians populate the rocks. Photographers will be happy to learn that the Garibaldis and senoritas are very cooperative. Expect to see horn sharks and yellowtails as well.

Game fish include lobster, halibut, and scallops, but do not touch! The area is a marine preserve, attracting a variety of creatures that aren't found elsewhere along the coast.

Rocky Beach is located south of Diver's Cove and Picnic Beach. Take Highway 1 through Laguna Beach. North of the center of town, turn onto Jasmine Street. There's metered parking along Cliff Drive. Two sets of stairs leading to the water's edge are located behind the shuffleboard and lawn bowling courts. Facilities at Heisler Park include showers, restrooms, and picnic areas.

Typical depth range:	10–40 feet
Access:	Stairs at base of Diamond Street; turn right off PCH
Water entry:	Sand with scattered rocks
Snorkeling:	Good to excellent
Rating:	Intermediate
Visibility:	15–45 feet

It's not unusual to see several hundred divers converge on the beaches in southern Orange County during the summer, particularly on weekends. To escape this madness, come to Wood's Cove. This spectacular dive site offers all the qualities you would expect to find in a Laguna Beach dive spot, without the crowds. It's located at the southern end of Laguna Beach about two miles down the coast from Diver's Cove and Shaw's Cove. Perhaps the most salient feature of Wood's Cove is its interesting bottom terrain. Two main reefs dominate the bottom. To the east, starting approximately 50 yards out is a reef made up of jumbled boulders and rock outcroppings. Water depths average 30–40 feet about 100 yards out and the reef reaches to within 15 feet to the surface in some spots. To the west there's a low-lying reef in 30 feet of water covered with kelp that sports an interesting feature: a huge boulder that rises to within a few feet of the surface. Take the opportunity to explore the overhangs created by the boulder.

Tunicates and anemones are commonly encountered by passing underwater photographers.

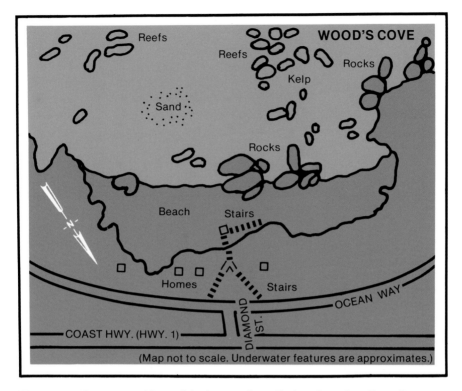

When many divers are rushing to join the crowds on the beaches of southern Orange County, others enjoy the solitude at Wood's Cove, a less-frequented site that offers a wide variety of diving pleasures.

There are other wonders in the area. On the east side of the cove, friendly Garibaldi will feed from your hands. There's also a colorful array of invertebrates on the rocks, including nudibranchs, anemones, gorgonians, and starfish, and, on the western reef, a small kelp forest. Unlike neighboring sites, Wood's Cove is not part of a marine reserve. Hunting is permitted as long as you follow California Fish and Game regulations. However, it's illegal to take abalone here. The lobster population is sparse except perhaps in the shallows. Small numbers of scallops are also present. Look on the outer reefs for kelp bass and sheepshead, and on the sand between the reefs for halibut.

To reach Wood's Cove, exit Highway 1 on Diamond Street. The stairs leading to the beach and cove are located at the intersection of Diamond and Ocean Way. There's limited parking along both roads. The stairway cuts through a garden separating private property, so please be considerate. The sandy beach on the cove is divided by a large boulder. The best spot to enter is to the left of the boulder on the east side of the cove. Beware of submerged rocks that break the surface at low tide. During the summer, a southerly swell can create difficult diving conditions.

Typical depth range:	10–60 feet
Access:	Stairs at Cleo Street; turn right off PCH
Water entry:	Sand with scattered rocks
Snorkeling:	Good to excellent
Rating:	Intermediate
Visibility:	15–20 feet

Cleo Street affords a sample of coastal wreck diving only a short distance from the beach. It is one of the only dive sites where a wreck can be accessed from shore. After making a sandy entry (watch out for the submerged rocks in the surf zone), divers can take a 220° compass heading towards the end of the kelp bed. The wreck sits along the outer perimeter of the kelp bed, and is easy to find. The Cleo Street wreck is really the barge *Foss 125,* which came to grief in foul weather in 1958. The barge is 130 feet in length, and is deteriorating rapidly.

Yet there is more to Cleo Street than the *Foss 125.* Kelp abounds in the area, as do calico bass, numerous lobster and small low-lying finger reefs covered with sea fans and anemones. Sheepshead are prominent throughout the kelp fronds, and rockfish and lingcod can be encountered as well. In the spring months, yellowtail and white seabass cruise the outer perimeter of the thick kelp bed, making it a favorite haunt among the spearfishing crowd.

Cleo Street Beach is not protected from incoming swells and is usually rougher than Shaw's and Diver's coves. But when calm, Cleo Street is well worth the effort. Whether you are inspecting the wreck or pursuing the marine life, it's a great dive when conditions permit. High tide conditions are usually best for this area. Divers should note that parking is limited (especially on weekends). It's a good idea to drop all gear and your diving partner off at the stairway and drive to any parking place available. Cleo Street is an excellent Laguna Beach dive site.

The Scripps aquarium is a terrific surface interval spot to visit when diving San Diego County.

Typical depth range:	10–35 feet
Access:	Stairs at Moss Street; turn right off PCH or Ocean Way
Water entry:	Sand with scattered rocks
Snorkeling:	Good to excellent
Rating:	Intermediate
Visibility:	15–25 feet

The cove at Moss Street offers diving pleasures that rival other locations in Laguna Beach—without the crowds. There are small walls and ledges to explore, rocks that tower 18 feet from the sandy bottom, and deep crevices that cut into the reef to form small caves. Conditions here are generally good all year. The cove is well protected, and currents usually affect only the extreme outer reef. Visibility averages 15–25 feet and can reach 35 feet under ideal conditions. Shallow parts of the reef are sometimes affected by surge. Avoid this area by moving to deeper waters 30–35 feet on the reef located 100–150 yards offshore.

Moss Street is located off Highway 1, approximately one mile south of the downtown area. Limited parking is available on Moss Street and nearby Ocean Way. If there are no parking spots, simply drop your gear at the top of the stairs and park a few blocks away. Be aware of the "No Parking" zones—they're everywhere! A short stairway leads to the small sandy beach. You can plan your dive from the top of the stairs. Note the rocks that break the surface on the south and northwest sides of the cove (at low tide). The rocks at the southern point, known as Moss Point, mark the beginning of the reef that interests most divers. There are reefs on the northwest side of the cove, but they're flat and lack the variety of marine life of the main reef.

These multi-armed sea stars are voracious predators of reef dwelling invertebrates.

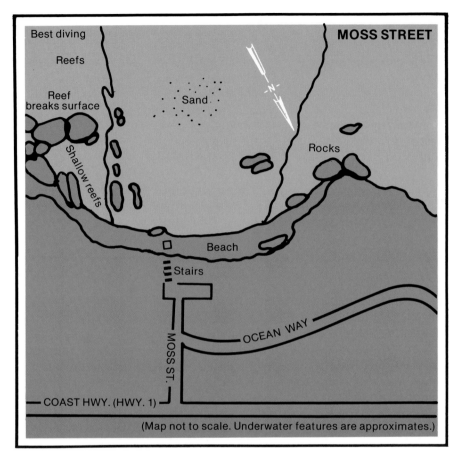

Moss Street is another less-frequented Laguna Beach dive site. Divers who enjoy walls and ledges, hunters, and photographers will find this spot extraordinary.

Upon entering, the bottom drops 5–6 feet. Beware of loose stones in the surf. The shallow water close to the beach is perfect for snorkeling on very calm days. To get to the southern reef, stay to your left as you face the ocean. You can avoid most of the surge by dropping to the bottom just beyond the rocks that break the surface. Beyond these rocks, the reef breaks up into an array of interesting rock formations. On the other side of the reef, the rocks create impressive overhangs and huge crevices.

From about 50 yards from shore out to the seaward end of the reefs, gorgonians are plentiful—in some spots, a brilliant golden blanket of gorgonians adds bursts of color. Feather worms and colorful anemones should delight the photographer. Hunters won't be disappointed, either. Head for the outer reefs for big game fish, including halibut. Lobster (when in season), small scallops, sheepshead, and kelp bass are also available.

A diver looks for photographic subjects on an exceptionally clear day in a Palos Verdes kelp bed.

Typical depth range:	15–25 feet
Access:	Park at Aliso Pier lot
Water entry:	Sand
Snorkeling:	Poor
Rating:	Novice
Visibility:	15–20 feet

Aliso Beach is easily identified by its distinctive diamond-shaped pier where Aliso Creek runs off into the sea. Parking is plentiful because the pier is a popular site for fishermen, divers, surfers, and skim boarders. The area may appear desolate to the naked eye, but there are several offshore reefs a good swim seaward and north of the pier.

For divers desiring a good trek north of the pier, an area named Treasure Island awaits. This is a private beach, so access can only be made by walking in at the mean high tide mark. A private trailer park sits back from the sand. Treasure Island offers more reef systems, usually in the form of low-lying finger and patch reefs. These reefs can be very productive for lobster hunting from October to March. Spearfishermen will encounter healthy-sized bass. The ornate invertebrate life and sea stars on the rocky ledges make excellent underwater photographic opportunities. This is an area that is often overlooked, but worth inspecting. You'll probably be surprised!

A small green moray eel makes its home on an offshore reef.

Typical depth range:	15–25 feet
Access:	Take PCH turnoff to Dana Point Harbor; park at dead-end past *Pilgrim* sailing vessel
Water entry:	Small rocks
Snorkeling:	Poor
Rating:	Advanced
Visibility:	5–20 feet

San Juan Rocks is located offshore Dana Point's steep, massive headland. The area was immortalized historically in Richard Henry Dana's classic *Two Years Before the Mast,* where San Juan Capistrano Mission fathers traded tallow and hides to Yankee brigs by throwing the goods off the cliff to sailors waiting below. The hides were loaded onto ships by seaman like Dana. In fact, the replica bark, *Pilgrim,* berthed at this end of Dana Harbor, is named after the ship on which Dana sailed.

San Juan Rocks offers good diving, but fickle visibility. When offshore breezes create an upwelling effect, water clarity can improve a great deal. Divers should also be careful of the boat traffic coming out of Dana Point Harbor and mindful of longshore current conditions. Dana Point is a "rounding buoy" for migratory grey whales, and dolphin can often be spotted from the headlands above. The area is a favorite marine mammal observation point. On the swim out to San Juan Rocks, divers will encounter jack mackerel, opaleye, Garibaldi, kelp bass, and scallops. During season, divers can do well catching lobster here.

For the best sightseeing at Scotchman's Cove, stay close to the exposed offshore reef. There are large reef formations rising 20 feet from the bottom in some spots, and in the cracks and crevices, much colorful life thrives.

4

Diving in San Diego County

From Carlsbad to the northern outskirts of San Diego and several "sleeper" dive sites. Those divers who visit these areas are usually locals, while out-of-town divers visit more-frequented sites. The diving is spectacular, but visibility is usually marginal because of shoreline sediments, and at times, strong surf. Run off from numerous estuaries and wetland areas can add to reduced water clarity. But for those who venture into the "no man's land," rewards await. It is not a spectacular photographic area, but game is abundant because of the lack of diver traffic.

Some of the best diving is at offshore reefs, requiring a swim of a fourth of a mile out or more. These areas include San Onofre, Oceanside Pier, and Carlsbad State Beach. Many consider the best site in San Diego County to be Sea Cliff Park, known by the surfing community as Swamis. Consequently, surf here can be well shaped and large, so pick your day carefully. Extensive reef systems close to shore at Swamis make the trip worth the effort. San Elijo State Park features a great beach campground, but divers have to "punch out" through prevalent surf and swim a good distance to reach some of the best dive sites. There is also good diving in the Del Mar area, but remember, visibility can be marginal.

South of Del Mar is the northern border of San Diego and La Jolla Underwater Park, the *créme de la créme* of San Diego diving. The only marine life that may be taken from this area is abalone, clams, and lobster. The San Diego-La Jolla Ecological Reserve is located within the boundaries of the park, as well as popular dive sites such as La Jolla Shores and Canyon, Goldfish Point, and La Jolla Cove. The diving here is predictably good, but no marine life may be taken or disturbed in any way.

San Diego has a large and active diving population. On any weekend expect to see numerous divers and many diving classes in progress. Most of the area from shore offers exceptional terrain featuring rocky headlands

Diving along the San Diego coastline is varied. The experienced and beginner diver can find enjoyment, relaxation, and exhilaration in areas including San Onofre State Beach (32), Radiation Bay (33), Swamis (34), Cardiff State Beach (35), Sumner Canyon (36), La Jolla Shores (37), Goldfish Point (38), La Jolla Cove (39), Children's Pool (40), Hospital Point (41), Windansea (42), Point Loma Kelp Beds (43), and Imperial Beach (44). ▶

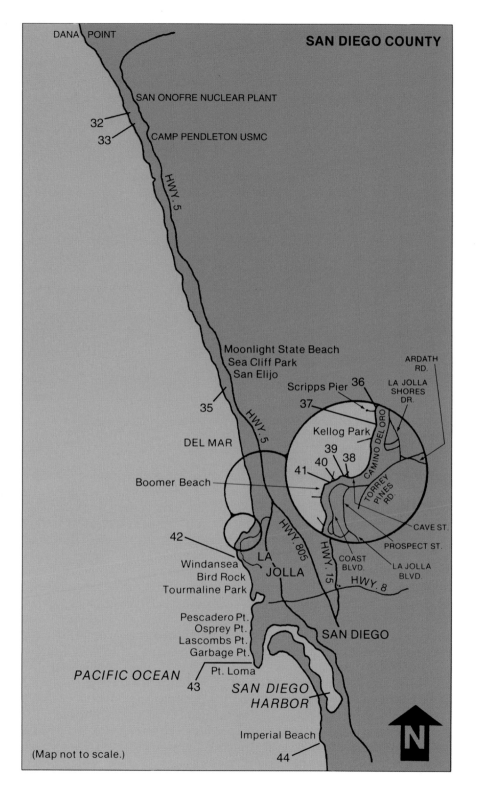

SAN DIEGO COUNTY

DANA POINT

SAN ONOFRE NUCLEAR PLANT

32

33

CAMP PENDLETON USMC

HWY. 5

Moonlight State Beach
Sea Cliff Park
San Elijo

Scripps Pier 36

37

ARDATH
RD.

LA JOLLA
SHORES
DR.

Kellog Park

35

HWY. 5

DEL MAR

39

40 38

Boomer Beach

41

CAMINO DEL ORO

TORREY PINES RD.

42

LA
JOLLA

HWY. 805

HWY. 15

CAVE ST.

PROSPECT ST.

COAST
BLVD.

LA JOLLA
BLVD.

HWY. 8

Windansea
Bird Rock
Tourmaline Park

Pescadero Pt.
Osprey Pt.
Lascombs Pt.
Garbage Pt.

SAN DIEGO

PACIFIC OCEAN

Pt. Loma

43

SAN DIEGO
HARBOR

N

Imperial Beach

44

(Map not to scale.)

Small boat diving is available off the beach in San Diego. Here divers launch an inflatable off La Jolla Shores.

and reefs and sandy plains. Small inflatable boats can even be launched directly off the sand at La Jolla Shores, affording beach divers a little bit of mobility, not to mention quick transport to their desired destinations.

San Diego diving is usually good, but don't expect spectacular visibility every day of the week. Conditions change from day to day. There may be 50-foot visibility on Saturday and 15-foot visibility on Sunday. You pay your money and take your chances.

Perhaps the most interesting feature in the La Jolla area is the presence of several submarine canyons. Here, divers can reach significant depths just by swimming from the shore. Watch your air supply and bottom time on these dives. San Diego deeper water experiences can be worthwhile, as a variety of marine creatures inhabit the canyons.

Overall, San Diego, especially the La Jolla area, offers phenomenal diving that is worth experiencing. An additional benefit to diving San Diego is there is so much to do on the surface, too. Visitors can stop off at the newly remodeled Scripps Aquarium, Seaworld, San Diego Wild Animal Park, or the 18th-century clipper ship *Star of India.* There are several motels and hotels in the San Diego area that can accommodate any budget. And don't forget, neighboring Mexico is only a short drive away.

Typical depth range:	15–35 feet
Access:	Off Highway 5 south of Basilione Road; north of nuclear reactor
Water entry:	Sand and small rocks
Snorkeling:	Poor
Rating:	Intermediate
Visibility:	5–15

Located near Camp Pendelton Marine Base and Southern California's only operational nuclear reactor, this is most commonly a surfing spot with reduced visibility. Yet it also remains a secret spot for lobster and scallops. The 3.5-mile area has a sandy beach below high bluffs. Paved paths allow divers to access the beach. Watch out for surfers when entering and exiting the water. Some facilities are located on the beach, but the coastline remains largely unspoiled.

Many divers venture to this area for the available game because it is often a good producer of lobster, scallops, and abalone. The only drawback to the area is the lack of visibility, but, with a sharp eye, lobster antennae can be found beneath the numerous low-lying rock piles.

San Onofre is a "sleeper" site for hunters because it is not often visited. Photography is generally poor in this area. The site features a small amount of kelp held fast to small patch reefs and rock piles. There is not much sand here as there are several cobblestones and sparse reefs. There are, however, large calico bass, as well as the usual complement of rock wrasse, senorita fish, and other indigenous marine critters.

The area here is really shallow, allowing divers an abundance of available bottom time. Try it some time! You may be surprised—after all, there is more to diving than crystal clear water. Some times surprises await in areas where water clarity is not the best.

Here is a close-up and personal look at corynactis anemones. These small but vibrant beauties dot most California reefs.

Typical depth range:	15–30 feet
Access:	South of San Onofre along the Coastal Access Road near the nuclear reactor
Water entry:	Small rocky beach
Snorkeling:	Poor
Rating:	Intermediate
Visibility:	10–15 feet

The name is merely a local joke. Don't worry about coming out of the water emanating a strange glow! This site is at the southern end of San Onofre State Beach, but deserves special mention. Rather than a long open area like Trestles (the northern surfing beach), Radiation Bay is a large cove surrounded by a steep marine terrace. There is more protection from wind and swell here, consequently, crowds of surfers and divers are often avoided. Conditions

A diver examines a small octopus.

A diver swims through one of the surge channels at Diver's Cove.

can be evaluated by standing on the bluff. If the northern end of San Onofre is undivable, or too crowded, Radiation Bay is a good bet.

Although the nuclear reactor is close by, divers do not need to check themselves for radiation doses after exiting the water.

The underwater terrain features a series of rambling finger and boulder reefs containing lobster, moray eels, Garibaldi, and a vibrant display of sea fans and anemones. It is not an underwater photographer's hot spot, but occasionally visibility can improve and the aquatic photogs can have a field day, but they to carry all of their heavy equipment down the long trail. When conditions are good, it is worth it.

This region is mostly an uncrowded area for sightseeing divers and hunters. Rock fish and calico bass are plentiful, and during the spring, white sea bass and yellow tail skirt the outer perimeter of the cove. A proficient hunter stands a decent chance at bagging these undersea delicacies. And don't forget the lobster and abalone either!

Despite the long walk, Radiation Bay has ample parking and restroom facilities at the top of the cliff. When conditions are good, you may want to give it a try.

Typical depth range:	15–40 feet
Access:	Stairs from First St. (old Hwy 101)
Water entry:	Mostly rocky
Snorkeling:	Great when calm
Rating:	Intermediate
Visibility:	15–35 feet

Moving farther south toward the Mexican border, off Santa Fe Drive in Encinitas, is Swamis, a stretch of beach venerated by divers and surfers alike. Swamis is south of the Self-Realization Ashram Center at Sea Cliff Roadside Park.

Avoid this area when surf is high, as the surge and the shallow rocky reefs are not a good combination (neither is the gaggle of surfboards in the water). When calm however, Swamis offers tremendous shallow water reef diving. The water can be sparkling clear and at times reveals a vibrant display of gorgonian fans, bright orange Garibaldi, anemones, and occasional nudibranchs. Sheepshead, calico bass, and varieties of perch grace the area as well.

Swamis terrain is unique and beautiful. The reefs are smooth and can often be seen from the stairs when water clarity is good. They are not traditional finger or boulder type reefs, but smooth solid rocks hosting the usual Southern California contingent of marine life. Anemones, sea fans, nudibranchs, sea urchins, and varieties of fish inhabit the slightly deeper reefs where surge is not as constant. During periods of large swell however, most fish head for deeper water and divers are advised to look for a cove elsewhere. Powerful surf can be dangerous. High surf, divers, and pointy surfboards are not a good combination. When the swell is slack, a visit to Swamis should be on every diver's underwater "hit list."

Bloodstars like these are found in differing hues from orange to vermilion.

Typical depth range:	20–40
Access:	Old Hwy 101 across San Elijo Lagoon
Water entry:	Sand
Snorkeling:	Fair
Rating:	Intermediate
Visibility:	10–20 feet

Located off old Highway 101, Cardiff Beach features a reef approximately one-fourth of a mile offshore. This is a predominantly sandy area that gives way to an extensive reef system. It's a bit of a swim, but worth it.

Many divers bypass Cardiff because of the expanse of sandy beach, not knowing that reefs await offshore. Although not frequented by underwater photographers, hunters may find scallops, a possible abalone or two, as well as the elusive lobster.

You have to search for the reef however. Take a compass heading seaward from San Elijo Lagoon and start looking. While swimming through the sand you'll find corbina, rays, sand sharks, and tube anemones. If you are lucky, a nice big halibut may be sitting in the sand waiting for you—don't confuse these fish with angel sharks however. Although angels are quite tasty, scientists speculate that they reproduce irregularly. It would be a shame to cull the resource faster than it can replenish itself. Many divers consider these gentle sharks more enjoyable to observe and photograph than to barbecue.

An area of Wood's Cove is covered in kelp. Don't miss the huge boulder around the kelp beds. It is an interesting spot to explore.

Typical depth range:	60–120 feet plus
Access:	Small boat access from La Jolla or private beach access through UCSD
Water entry:	Sand and small rocks
Snorkeling:	Poor
Rating:	Advanced
Visibility:	10–50 feet

Perhaps the most spectacular of San Diego's submarine canyons, Sumner does not have the easiest access to the general public. An inflatable can be launched from nearby La Jolla Shores and divers can race north of La Jolla to access the area in minutes. Divers can also make a *long* walk from the pier parking lot and make a *long* swim from shore, or, on rare occasions, access from the University of California at San Diego can be granted and divers can strike out from shore. A small inflatable run from La Jolla Shores (inflatables can be launched from the beach here) in generally easiest.

Sumner canyon is made up of a sandstone wall that plummets seaward at approximately 50 feet. Attainable depths descend well beyond recreational diving limits, but a diver with good buoyancy control can enjoy this California coastal wall by dangling his fins over hundreds of feet of blue water while inspecting the marine life growing on the wall itself. Because the wall is sandstone, its soft escarpment encourages an unusual variety of deep water dwellers. Yellow and pink branching corals sweep out into the current. Colonies of pink and purple corynactis anemones carpet the wall, while skittish calico bass dart off into deeper depths. Occasionally large torpedo rays are encountered cruising off the sandy ledges in search of prey.

Visibility can vary, and because the wall is not coral lined in nature, its soft sediments can easily be stirred up, obscuring visibility.

The use of a surface float and ascent line (if diving off an inflatable boat, the anchor line works fine) is recommended to make a controlled safety stop on the way back to the surface. Remember Sumner gets deep quick, so use caution when planning your dive to stay within proper depth and air supply limits. On a good day, when care is exercised, Sumner Canyon is one of San Diego County's best.

California sea lions are not usually encountered off local beaches except for some remote areas along Palos Verdes and south Orange County. ▶

Typical depth range:	40–120 feet plus
Access:	Park area north of Vallecitos St.
Water entry:	Sandy beach
Snorkeling:	Poor
Rating:	Novice to advanced
Visibility:	10–30 feet

"The training ground for the San Diego diver" is how one diver described this area after stepping from the surf at La Jolla shores.

What makes La Jolla Canyon a perennial favorite of local divers at all skill levels? The answers range from good facilities to easy surf entry and excellent shore access. But let's not forget the spectacular scenery. Approximately 100 yards from shore in 35–70 feet of water, the ocean floor breaks into a steep vertical wall that extends to depths of over 800 feet.

Access to the submarine canyon is from the beach of La Jolla Shores located north of La Jolla Bay. The beach offers excellent facilities and ample parking. The best point for water entry is directly off a small lifeguard tower marked #20. The tower is located south of the main lifeguard tower that's positioned at the front of the park and slightly north of Vallecitos Street. Surfers congregate north of the main tower. Stay clear of this area, as well as the area near the boat ramp, located south of Vallecitos Street at the end of Aveinda de La Playa.

As you move out from tower #20, the sandy bottom slopes moderately. Go out about 100 yards from the tower, then line yourself up so that the end of Scripp's Pier (to the north) is directly under the green building that's located on the ridge. This will place you slightly inshore from the rim of canyon in about 40 feet of water. At 50 feet there's a series of ledges that vary in height from 10–20 feet. The bottom drops off quickly to more than 300 feet. It's an exhilarating feeling to position yourself on the rim of the canyon and peer into the depths. Visibility averages 15–20 feet but can worsen with heavy surf or when plankton blooms. If there are upwellings from the canyon, visibility can improve to 30–40 feet. These upwellings also bring marine animals from the deeper waters to the rim for closer observation. Squid appear in late fall and early spring, and they in turn attract other large fish.

Several varieties of small colorful fish can be found on the clay canyon walls. Small branches of gorgonian are attached to the ledges at 65 feet, while crabs and octopuses make their homes in the holes in the clay walls. Look but don't touch! The entire area is an underwater park and ecological preserve. Marine life may not be removed or disturbed.

After you dive, feel free to freshen up at the outdoor freshwater showers located in the restroom building just behind tower #20. Then enjoy a picnic lunch in the park.

Typical depth range:	15–30 feet
Access:	Stairs and path; parking lot by Cave St.
Water entry:	Rocky entry
Snorkeling:	Good
Rating:	Novice to intermediate
Visibility:	15–30 feet

Named for the Garibaldi that congregate in the area, Goldfish Point is located at the tip of a peninsula that lies between La Jolla Cove and La Jolla

Goldfish Point is named for the abundant Garibaldi in the area. Although marine life is plentiful, divers must abide by the La Jolla Underwater Park rules, which prohibit the taking or disturbing of any marine organisms.

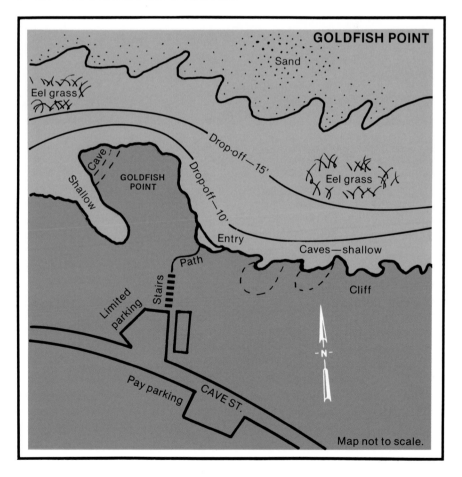

A successful underwater hunter bags a spiny lobster. Be sure to measure all game underwater and bring only legal-sized dinners home.

Caves on the southern end of La Jolla Bay. The fish have grown accustomed to the divers and are always looking for handouts. If you're carrying food, don't be surprised if you're stalked by one of these friendly animals. Be aware that Goldfish Point is part of the La Jolla Underwater Park. You're not permitted to remove or disturb any marine life. However, feel free to observe lobster, octopus, and other shy creatures!

For the photographer, starfish and anemones provide a colorful background, and the variable bottom presents some splendid photo opportunities. Reefs covered with eel grass drop to a sandy bottom 50 yards out. There are also ledges and sand channels for you to explore.

There are two ways to access the diving area adjacent to the point. The most direct route is via a path located behind the La Jolla Cave Curio Shop. A stairway and short, steep path lead to a small rock shelf at the water's edge. This is a good spot for entries, but only during very calm weather. You can also enter at La Jolla Cove and swim 200 yards to the point. There's an underground parking lot located across from the Curio Shop. Parking fees aren't cheap, but it beats driving around for hours looking for a parking spot.

Typical depth range:	15–30 feet
Access:	Limited parking in front of Scripps Memorial Park
Water entry:	Sandy beach
Snorkeling:	Good
Rating:	Novice to intermediate
Visibility:	10–30 feet

La Jolla Cove is another popular spot, favored by divers and beach goers. Consequently, if you want to dive this area on summer weekends, be prepared to deal with the crowds. The cove lies on the northernmost extension of the La Jolla Peninsula. Because the cove faces north, it's well protected from the southerly swells that affect the area during the summer.

One diver assists several others as they make a rocky beach exit. Rocky entry and exits are simple and safe when approached cautiously.

A spiraling kelp stipe unfolds newly grown leaves. Kelp is the fastest growing plant in the world.

There's a series of rock ledges, reefs, and sand channels directly out from the small sandy cove. Around the point to the northwest, in an area known as "Alligator Head," marine life is abundant. Garibaldi are everywhere and, if you're lucky, you may spot a broomtail grouper. Seals are also frequent visitors, and they've grown accustomed to the divers. Moray eels, lobster, and rockfish can be found on the bottom and in the reefs. Keep in mind that La Jolla Cove lies within the San Diego-La Jolla Underwater Ecological Reserve. Do not remove or disturb the marine life.

On the other side of the cove, a series of rock ledges stretch close to the shore all the way to Goldfish Point. The water depth here is 30 feet. Farther out in deeper water, the bottom turns to sand where you'll find angel sharks and halibut.

Because of the crowds, it may be difficult to find a parking spot. Your best bet is to dive early in the morning or on a weekday. Parking adjacent to the Ellen Browning Scripps Memorial Park, which overlooks the cove, is limited. There are no parking meters but there is a three-hour time limit. The park offers all the amenities you'll need for post-diving activities: restrooms, showers, telephones, picnic areas, and large grassy areas for suiting up. Water and surf conditions are posted daily at the lifeguard stand. It's advisable to check the diving conditions before you arrive. Although the cove is protected, large surf and surge are not uncommon.

The best spot to enter the water is from the small sandy beach in the middle of the cove. There are two entry points to avoid: "the hole," an indentation in the cliffs on the east side of the cove that generates rips and unpredictable currents, and a dangerous shallow reef farther to the east.

A small, calm bay near La Jolla Cove, Children's Cove is a good area for beginner divers or snorkelers. On land, facilities are well-equipped. ▶

Children's Pool (Casa Pool) 40

Typical depth range:	10–30 feet
Access:	Ramps and stairway off Coast Blvd.
Water entry:	Sandy beach
Snorkeling:	Good
Rating:	Novice
Visibility:	10–30 feet

Children's Pool is located less than a half mile south of La Jolla Cove along Coast Boulevard. This manmade cove, also known as Casa Pool, was carved out at a spot that's protected from the swells by a small sea wall, creating a pool of ocean water for children to play in. This is an excellent spot for divers to enter to reach the nearby reefs.

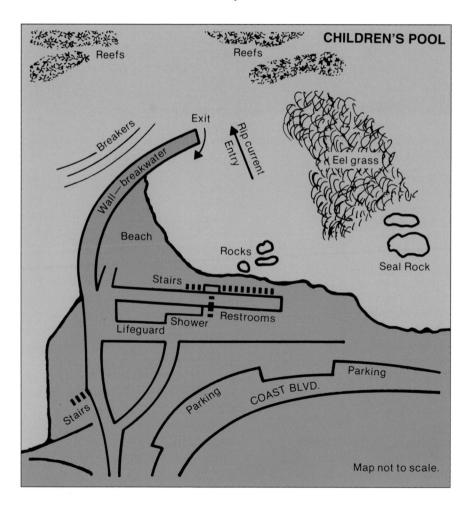

CHILDREN'S POOL

Reefs

Reefs

Exit

Breakers

Wall – breakwater

Rip current

Entry

Eel grass

Beach

Rocks

Seal Rock

Stairs

Restrooms

Shower

Lifeguard

Parking

Stairs

Parking

COAST BLVD.

Parking

Map not to scale.

Entry into normally clear and calm waters makes scuba diving and snorkeling at Casa Pool very popular.

Depths on the reefs range from 10–30 feet. Extreme undercutting has created huge rock ledges which are inhabited by a variety of marine life. Eel grass is abundant in the shallow portions. Anemones, sponges, starfish, nudibranchs, and a variety of mollusks can be found on the ledges and rocks. Expect to find Garibaldi, senoritas, opaleye, and other fish on the reefs. You may also spot a grouper, and seals are frequent visitors. Lobster and abalone can sometimes be found on the outer reefs, in addition to sheepshead, calico bass, halibut, and white sea bass.

Enter Children's Pool from the small sandy beach. The strong rip running out from the end of the wall will get you to the reefs rather quickly. Returning to the cove is best done by swimming very close to the tip of the wall, where the surge will push you back into the cove. Water conditions are posted daily at the lifeguard tower.

Parking along Coast Boulevard is limited and restricted to three hours. To avoid the crowds, schedule your dive for the early morning or on a weekday. Restrooms, showers, and a drinking fountain are located below the lifeguard tower; telephones can be found behind the tower.

Typical depth range:	10–35 feet
Access:	Stair ½ mile south of Children's Pool off Coast Blvd.
Water entry:	Sandy beach
Snorkeling:	Fair
Rating:	Intermediate
Visibility:	10–25 feet

Hospital Point, sometimes called Whale View Point, is a large rocky area located less than one-half mile south of Children's Pool. There are a number of possible entry points along the rocky shore, but the one most widely used by local divers is across from 417 Coast Boulevard. A short stairway leads to a small sandy beach, where you'll enter. Especially when the surf is up, water entry can be difficult when the shallow reefs are exposed at low tide. Channels also create rips. Diving is best done at high tide.

The bottom is very shallow until about 40 yards out, where a ledge marks the drop into deeper water. The bottom gradually slopes down to 40 feet approximately 300 yards from shore. A collection of reefs interspersed with sand channels, most of which run parallel to shore, rise 10 feet above the bottom. One features a small arch you can swim through.

Even with moderate surf, surge can be a problem. You can avoid some effects of the surge by staying low in the channels between the reefs. Under good conditions, visibility averages 15–30 feet. Morays, bottom fish, octopus, lobster, and abalone can be found on the bottom offshore of the point.

Except on crowded days, parking isn't usually a problem. There are no facilities, but you'll find a few picnic tables and barbecue pits nearby.

A photographer's strobe is placed behind the subject to backlight this gorgonian sea fan.

Typical depth range:	15–35 feet
Access:	West of Neptune Place near Nautilus St.
Water entry:	Rocky and sandy beach
Snorkeling:	Good
Rating:	Intermediate to advanced
Visibility:	15–40 feet when calm

Windansea features an extensive reef 500 feet from shore. Occasionally big surf breaks in this area, but when calm it offers spectacular diving and snorkeling. Visibility can be quite spectacular when conditions permit, so plan your expedition accordingly. Avoid Windansea when the surf is large, as it can become a dangerous place where waves and divers collide.

The reefs are quite colorful, and sometimes surfers can see the bottom while sitting on their boards at the surface. Of course, the view is much better for divers. Sea fans, anemones, branching corals, and nudibranch all await. Filter-feeding barnacles and scallops grow on the reef substrate, and diver may encounter lobster and eel in the crevices. Needless to say, on a clear day underwater photography is excellent here.

It is a good idea to check with local weather reports before driving to the area, and then evaluate conditions before suiting up. If the area is not divable, another nearby cove may be.

Kids often play in the tide pool at Scripps Beach, San Diego, near Sumner Canyon and the Scripps Pier.

Typical depth range:	30–110 feet
Access:	Best by small boat
Water entry:	Boat
Snorkeling:	Good (in the surface kelp)
Rating:	Advanced
Visibility:	20–60 feet plus

The Point Loma kelp beds are probably one of the most picturesque diving areas in San Diego. Few divers access the area by shore, but a quick trip in a small boat out of San Diego Bay allows divers to float through this majestic undersea forest after a short ride.

This area features terrain and marine life similar to what one would expect to find off California's offshore islands. There are large reef systems with kelp plants towering high above. Divers will encounter sea stars, nudibranch, anemones, bright orange Garibaldi and calico bass. Additionally, it is not uncommon to observe the occasional migratory grey whale on the kelp perimeters, as well as pelagic blue sharks gliding off in the distance. A dedicated hunter can find yellowtail racing along the fringes of Point Loma during spring and summer months.

Inside the kelp beds, divers will encounter lobster, Pacific electric rays, and varieties of crab. The kelp system itself provides habitat for myriads of juvenile fish.

Point Loma's Kelp Beds give photographers an excellent opportunity to stalk and shoot numerous sea creatures. During periods of surf and swell, visibility in the area is not its best, but when calm prevails (and an upwelling helps too) visibility can be staggering, even exceeding the 60-foot mark. If you haven't visited this area, make it a point to do so soon. A tremendous undersea menagerie awaits those who come to dive and enjoy this spectacular undersea hanging garden.

Dawn's promise: a rainbow at the Point Loma lighthouse in San Diego.

97

Typical depth range:	15–30 feet
Access:	5 Freeway, exit right on Coronado Ave.
Water entry:	Sand
Snorkeling:	Poor
Rating:	Very advanced
Visibility:	5–15 feet or less

Sand as far as the eye can see, but there's more. The most interesting aspect of this beach that stretches out just before reaching the Mexican border is a deteriorating United States Navy World War I vintage submarine—the *S-37*. It lies in the surf zone and is difficult to find from the beach. Divers embarking in beachcombing exploration can find portions of the wreck awash during very low tides.

The fact that the submarine is so shallow, and may often have waves breaking on or near it, means it is not often dived. Visibility is usually marginal, but on calm days, divers using small boats, or striking out from the beach, can access the wreck and experience 10–15 feet of water clarity.

Many artifacts have been removed from the submarine over the years, and it is heavily encrusted with barnacles and other marine invertebrates. Lobsters are often found in the sand at the base of the wreck, or inside. Salvage divers cut a large hole into the sub, but penetrating the wreck is not advised except for those who have extensive experience in shipwreck or cave penetration. (Even then, the deterioration poses risks that are better avoided.) The interior of the submarine is full of sand and sediment, so visibility inside becomes quickly obscured upon entry. This class of submarine allows little room for ease of interior entry and mobility. For those experienced in this type of diving (and who enjoy it), an Imperial Beach foray to the *S-37* can be exciting, but remember to be cautious.

Other than the submarine wreck, Imperial Beach is a sand dive with limited visibility, but sand bass and halibut may be found for those willing to cruise the seemingly barren desert in search of game. Beyond Imperial Beach lies Tijuana Slough and slightly farther south, the United States and Mexican border. As the last bastion of U.S. coastal diving in Southern California, San Diego County fails to disappoint.

A diver is suspended along the vertical section of the wall at Deadman's Reef, Laguna Beach. ▶

5

Safety

Diving the Los Angeles-Orange-San Diego County areas along California's coast can be a safe and enjoyable experience. Be sure to evaluate conditions before going in the water and heed the cautions listed for each individual dive site. It is important to remember that nothing is 100 percent safe, and divers must be responsible for making the right decisions and avoiding error. There are, however, a few guidelines that should be elaborated upon to help.

Proper Weighting. Unfortunately, many divers venture seaward with more lead on their belts than they really need. This causes stress and discomfort. Be sure you are using the proper amount of weight that is right for you, and remember, just because you learned to dive with a certain amount of weight doesn't mean you can use less as you become a more relaxed and proficient diver.

Buoyancy Control. This relates to proper weighting also. If divers cannot control their ascents and descents, they may find themselves stuck on the bottom or ascending too quickly. Swim to the surface slowly and vent air from your BC and don't use your power inflator on ascent. When you are venturing to deeper depths, be sure to inflate your vest to maintain neutral buoyancy. Fine tune your buoyancy control throughout the dive.

Hypothermia. Diving in California is cold. Occasionally divers get too cold. When the body gets numb, so does the brain. If you find yourself shivering uncontrollably, get out of the water and get warm. San Diego is known for its colder waters.

Surf and rocky entries. These usually appear to be trickier than they actually are. Still, no one wants to crash onto a rock or get pounded in the surf zone. Gauge your entries and exits carefully. Timing is important when water is rising or falling quickly.

Hazardous Marine Animals. Most marine critters are docile. However, you can hurt yourself by coming in contact with sea urchins. They are not attack-trained, but if you crash into one it can be painful. Moray eels are docile until harassed. Don't stick your hand in a crevice—a moray may bite. Stingrays can deliver a powerful barbed lash if stepped on. These animals inhabit the sandy plains, so it's a good idea to shuffle your fins during entry and exit to let them know you are coming so they get out of the way. Rockfish and scorpion fish have spines that can deliver a venomous sting if you place your hand on one.

Steer clear of the bold and aggressive Pacific electric ray (a.k.a. torpedo ray). These cousins to sharks are curious and often swim right up to divers. Don't pet one however; they pack a significant wallop. Their frontal lobes can deliver quite an electric shock.

Diving Accidents: Orange to San Diego Counties. Using the California-wide 911 number is not the best option in a diving accident where decompression sickness or an air embolism may be suspected, but it is recommended for life threatening trauma and "slip and fall" problems.

For this region, the following phone numbers are most effective should a serious diving incident occur:

Medical Alert Center (MAC)

(213) 221-4114

U.S. Coast Guard Emergency Coordination Center

(310) 590-2225

Divers Alert Network (DAN)

(919) 684-2948

Be certain to inform your point of contact that this is a diving related accident. Give your location and stand by for further instructions.

And Finally. Know your personal diving skill limitations! Don't jump into the ocean on a day you don't feel up to it, or at a site that is really out of your league. If you are new to diving these areas (and are unsure of your abilities in this environment), contact a local instructor or a divemaster for an orientation to the area.

Additionally, always plan and execute your dive within preset, predive parameters. Discuss depth, time, and air supply limits with your diving partner.

Weather Information

Perhaps one of the best methods for determining how weather will affect an area dive site is by watching local television news. Satellite maps are invaluable for predicting approaching offshore storms and low pressure fronts as well as favorable high pressure systems and offshore winds. The only drawback is that many television surf reports miss the accuracy mark. Confirm what you see on the weather report with the following telephone information systems:

Offshore weather from Monterey to the Mexican border
(213) 477-1463
Huntington Beach surf report
(714) 536-9303
Newport Beach surf report
(714) 673-3371
Laguna Beach surf and dive report
(714) 494-6573
San Diego surf and dive report
(619) 225-9492

The surf reports are often recorded by beach lifeguards and updated throughout the day. Water clarity and diving conditions may be included, as well as height and direction of swell.

Rocky reefs are habitat for several colorful fish such as this sheepshead. However, good access for shore diving requires a bit of effort and gear hauling.

Appendix

Diving Operations

Marina Del Rey Divers
2539 Lincoln Blvd.
Marina Del Rey
(213) 827-1131

American Diving
1901 Pacific Coast Hwy.
Lomita
(213) 326-6663

Dive N' Surf
504 W. Broadway
Redondo Beach
(213) 372-8423

Blue Cheer
1110 Wilshire Blvd.
Santa Monica
(213) 828-1217

Malibu Divers
21231 Pacific Coast Hwy
Malibu
(213) 456-2396

Scuba Haus
2501 Wilshire Blvd.
Santa Monica
(213) 828-2916

Reef Seekers Dive Co.
8542 Wilshire Blvd.
Beverly Hills
(310) 652-4990

Sea D' Sea
1911 Catalina Ave.
Redondo Beach
(310) 373-6355

Marina Dive & Sport
141 West 22nd St.
San Pedro
(310) 831-5647

Sport Chalet Divers
920 Foothill Blvd.
La Canada
(818) 790-9800

Sport Chalet Divers
24200 W. Lyons Ave.
Valencia
(805) 253-3883

Scuba Duba Dive
7126 Reseda Blvd.
Reseda
(818) 881-4545

Scuba Luv
22725 Ventura Blvd.
Woodland Hills
(818) 346-4799

Pacific Scubanaut
6959 Van Nuys Blvd.
Van Nuys
(818) 787-7066

West Coast Divers Supply
16931 Sherman Way
Van Nuys (818) 708-8136/8137

Desert Scuba
44441 N. Sierra Hwy. 6
Lancaster
(805) 948-8883

Sport Chalet Divers
Media City Center
Burbank
(818) 558-3500

Ciburdi Scuba Center
2272 Michelson Dr.
Irvine
(714) 955-1446

Divers Corner
12045 Paramount Blvd.
Downey
(213) 869-7702

New England Divers
4148 Viking Way
Long Beach
(213) 421-8939 or (714) 827-5110

Gucciones Scuba Habitat
2843 #A Diamond Bar Blvd.
Diamond Bar
(714) 594-7927

Pasadena Scuba & Travel
2848 E. Foothill Blvd.
Pasadena
(818) 796-2000

Diver's West
2333 E. Foothill Blvd.
Pasadena
(818) 796-4287

Southern California Diving Center
1121 S. Glendora Ave.
West Covina
(818) 338-8863

Sport Diving West
11501 Whittier Blvd.
Whittier
(213) 692-7373

Pacific Wilderness & Ocean Sports
1719 S. Pacific Ave
San Pedro
(213) 833-2422

Adventure Dive Center
1451 W. Arrow Hwy.
San Dimas
(714) 599-1997

Aquatic Image Expeditions
2355 Foothill Blvd. #261
La Verne 91750
(818) 852-2028

Sarcas Ski & Sport
2451 #B Foothill Blvd.
La Verne
(714) 596-4946

Antelope Valley Scuba
1430 W. Ave. I
Antelope Valley
(805) 949-2555

Adventures in Diving
31678 Pacific Coast Hwy.
Laguna Beach
(714) 499-4517

Aquatic Center
4535 Pacific Coast Hwy.
Newport Beach
(714) 650-5440

Black Bart's
24882 Muirlands
El Toro
(714) 855-2323

Black Bart's
34145 Pacific Coast Hwy.
Dana Point
(714) 946-5891

Openwater Habitat
411 South Main St.
Orange
(714) 744-8355

Scuba World
1706 N. Tustin
Orange
(714) 998-6383

Sport Chalet Divers
2500 E. Imperial Hwy.
Brea
(714) 225-0132

Sport Chalet Divers
16242 Beach Blvd.
Huntington Beach
(714) 848-0988

Sport Chalet Divers
27551 Puerta Real
Mission Viejo
(714) 582-3363

W.E.T.
20 National Blvd
National City
(619) 477-DIVE

W.E.T.
2525 Morena Blvd.
San Diego
(619) 275-1822

The Dive Center
2963 Carlsbad Blvd.
Carlsbad
(619) 729-0808

Sport Chalet Divers
4313 La Jolla Village Dr.
San Diego
(619) 552-0712

Sport Chalet Divers
5500 Grossmont Center
La Mesa
(619) 463-9381

Sport Chalet Divers
3695 Midway Drive
San Diego
(619) 224-6777

Del Mar Ocean Sports
1227 Camino Del Mar
Del Mar
(619) 792-1903

Diving Locker
1020 Grand
San Diego
(619) 272-1120

Diving Locker
8650 Miramar #C
San Diego
(619) 271-5231

Diving Locker
405 N. Hwy 101
Solana Beach
(619) 755-6822

Ocean Enterprises
7710 Balboa Ave.
San Diego
(619) 565-6054

Ocean Enterprises
1403 Encinitas Blvd.
Encinitas
(619) 942-3661

Pacific Coast Divers
3809 Plaza
Oceanside
(619) 726-7060

Rick's Diving Locker
945 W. Valley Parkway
Escondido
(619) 746-8980

Index

 **Pisces Books™**

Be sure to check out these other great books from Pisces:

Great Reefs of the World
Watching Fishes: Understanding Coral Reef Fish Behavior
Skin Diver Magazine's Book of Fishes, 2nd Edition
Shooting Underwater Video: A Complete Guide to the Equipment and Techniques
    for Shooting, Editing, and Post-Production

Diving and Snorkeling Guides to:

Australia: Coral Sea and Great Barrier Reef
Australia: Southeast Coast and Tasmania
The Bahamas: Family Islands and Grand Bahama
The Bahamas: Nassau and New Providence Island 2nd Edition
Belize
Bonaire
The British Virgin Islands
The Cayman Islands 2nd Edition
The Channel Islands
Cozumel, 2nd Edition
Curaçao
Fiji
Florida's East Coast, 2nd Edition
The Florida Keys, 2nd Edition
The Great Lakes
The Hawaiian Islands, 2nd Edition
Northern California and the Monterey Peninsula, 2nd Edition
The Pacific Northwest
Roatan and Honduras' Bay Islands
Texas
The Turks and Caicos Islands
The U.S. Virgin Islands, 2nd Edition